# STRIKE THE RIGHT CHORD

A DIY GUIDE TO GLOBAL SUCCESS IN TODAY'S
MUSIC INDUSTRY

PAUL SPENCER ALEXANDER

# INTRODUCTION

*You are the master of your future.* Maybe you haven't always felt that way. And maybe you've been told by friends or others in the music industry, and even your family, that there's no future in being a singer, songwriter or musician. Perhaps you've been given very discouraging advice, warning you that "you'll waste your whole life and still never get anywhere with your music and you'll likely starve along the way."

That's pretty negative "advice," isn't it? But if you've braved through those harsh words, since you chose music—or music *chose you*, then congratulations...you are exactly the person I've written *Strike the Right Chord* for.

This book is different than other guidebooks on becoming successful in music. It enables you to gain global success from your home computer. While many guidebooks show you how to distribute your music online, nothing will happen if it just sits in cyberspace without an ongoing promotional strategy.

*Strike the Right Chord* allows you to take a do-it-yourself approach to establishing yourself in the music world, showing you how to get started in the *right* direction toward success. It doesn't just teach you how to copyright, upload, and distribute your music online. It teaches you how to make your music *sell*—gain visibility—*where* to go online to *automate* the promotion of your songs while you learn to build your music company—*how* to name your songs in a way that accesses music fans who might not normally listen to your musical style—and *gain* them as fans anyway.

In this global music industry, the ability to *connect* with music fans and music companies worldwide from your home computer—and knowing *where* to go online—is what it *truly* means to "strike the right chord."

If you're brand-new to the industry, you'll find everything here to get started. Already established and looking to do more? I've got the info here to take everything to the next level. You can jump in anywhere you'd like.

I've laid out all the steps to your music success in 3 easy sections: *Getting Started, The Business of Music, and Going Further*, with a bonus section, *Managing Life—and Time—Along the Way.*

In *Getting Started*, I'll take you through the most important, first step: creating your music. After all, without a music product to sell, you don't have a business! I will help you discover the right name for yourself and your songs, teaching you how to record and master your music in top-quality—even on a *very* little budget. I will cover copyrighting your music, legal assistance and other basics centered around the creation of your music.

*The Business of Music* is where things really begin to take off for you! This section will teach you how to start your own production company and establish you in the music industry. You will learn about licenses and legal entities, logo creation and creating a website for sales and visibility. I'll provide detailed strategies on uploading your music to various streaming services, how you get paid for streaming and downloads, the ideal product formats for today's digital music landscape and options for distributing your music around the globe.

Once you've completed these essential tasks, it's time to move on to my next section on *Going Further*. Here, you'll learn how to make social media work for you, how to earn money making music videos, how to create a music video or short musical film that can be submitted to international film festivals, secrets to creating a video presence on no budget and using services like YouTube to broadcast your music video. You will also receive the best performance tips for a *winning* live show that takes over the venue.

You'll learn about record pools in the digital music age, creating an electronic press kit and how to target them to the right companies so you can increase sales, how to automate your publicity online, when to seek out public relations firms, agents, managers and, most importantly, how to access and succeed with your music in the global media—the same way big businesses do—using just your home computer.

I'll also teach you how to get your songs reviewed and embedded for paid streaming on thousands of potential music blogs, with links to your actual music product for sale. You'll learn about music merchandising for additional income, how to access and correctly approach global record labels (databases of these global record labels are provided) and how to communicate with them for successful consideration, using your electronic press kit.

I'll show you how you can enter the lucrative world of music licensing—with so many other websites where you can publish your music news and make your music career grow—*all* from your home computer!

This is a book you can share with your family and friends, showing them that it is *possible* to succeed in music, even asking them to help you and be proud of you along this journey. My goal is to help you turn your passion into a personal and professional victory. I want to root you on! Please feel free to email me at: email.psalexander@gmail.com and tell me your success stories, your challenges, your "aha" moments, the peaks, and the valleys.

All the best in music and success,

Paul Spencer Alexander

This book is dedicated to Singer-Songwriters, Songwriters, Musicians, and any Musical Talent from all backgrounds and upbringings, with a particular compassion for those who might share a deeply rooted and specific emotional pain of not previously being able to develop their natural musical talents to their full potential and launch a successful music career. One of the principle reasons this tragedy might exist is because their budding musical talents were often presented to parents or mentors whose worst fear was that their child would be "throwing their life away" or "risking a life of poverty and suffering" if they ever went into anything concerning the arts. These parents love their children and want to protect them, as good parents do. Unfortunately, in an effort that could be described as tough-love-gone wrong, they may have been too harsh, or dismissive, or even verbally abusive—either undermining their child's musical gifts by telling them they weren't any good when they were good, or using comments like, "You're dreaming" or "Stop dreaming," and speaking in a very cruel tone at a time when children should be dreaming.

This is a book you can share with your family and friends, showing them that it is possible to succeed in music—even asking them to help you and be proud of you along your journey. I have written and curated it to provide everything a music artist needs to become successful, both professionally and personally.

*Whether a child has now reached the age of 18 or 60, they have often suffered a cognitive dissonance and sadness where being told to "wake up and get a real job" is constantly in conflict with their musical calling—causing them to struggle and feel like failures at the notion of doing either.*

*The internal conflict gets in the way too much, and self-esteem dangerously suffers in all areas of their lives because, despite the parents' or mentors' best efforts to guide the child in what they believed was the right direction, the methods, tactics and tones they used might have made the child grow up feeling unloved or unworthy. Some of these adult children experienced arrested development, made poor choices when choosing friends, and have never been able to get their lives balanced and working correctly. This book is designed to assist in turning this tragedy into a personal or professional victory for each and every one of these musical children, including the grown-up ones.*

*That's the heart of this book—and it is dedicated to you, dear artist.*

# I

---

# CREATING YOUR MUSIC

# 1

## THE NAME OF YOUR SONG MAKES A HUGE DIFFERENCE

Naming your songs, and the use of (maybe surprising) keywords, will put you at a *huge* advantage in gaining attention for you and your music—far beyond what you might think.

> ***Take Note:*** Don't worry, I will not be teaching you anything that suggests you alter your actual songs or musical material. That's the beauty of it. Your completed work is your completed work.

Some of the following information can be used in all online marketing, but in this chapter, we focus on online digital music streaming services/digital music sales platforms. How you name your songs, as well as the keyword suggestions I point out, can:

- Dramatically increase your streams and sales across multiple digital music platforms.
- Provide you with superior online ingestion.
- Heighten music industry interest in you.

- Bring you increased press attention and fan visibility.

This chapter will teach you:

- The importance of the name for your music.
- How to use names to tell fans what to expect in your music.
- How to use keywords in names to help fans find your music in searches.
- How using the correct terms for your genre can generate more interest from micro-targeted, niche music fans actively looking for *your* musical style—and even those *not* necessarily looking for your style.
- The importance of using the correct terms and keywords where you might choose to name your musical materials, singles or albums differently, so that when these niche music lovers go searching for your style, you may pop up higher than other artists who have *not* learned these secrets.

Using these strategies, you end up potentially getting paid *more* for a larger number of streams of your song by people searching in your genre—and those *not* searching in your genre.

I would feel remiss if I did not explain the importance of getting your songs properly *named*—so they receive the biggest chance of increasing possible sales and streams across major retailers online.

As I said above, the information I am about to share is not meant to persuade you to alter any of your titles in any way. As an artist myself, who has been around the block in music, music publishing and music-related films and awards, I am the *last* person who would ever want you to compromise the names of your titles. However, the reality is, in terms of potentially increasing music sales, sometimes you *should* rename your songs. Whether to do so is entirely up to you.

If you do choose to rename your songs, the naming and keyword strategies below will help you reach even people who are not fans of your musical style but might be intrigued enough to listen to your song. And you will get paid for the stream even if the listener does not become a fan of yours, although there is always a chance that they will *become* fans. I will also be discussing in later chapters how these naming strategies are instrumental in increasing your visibility and sales on all digital sales and distribution platforms.

Music fans are often more diverse in their musical tastes than we can imagine. This is where you come in. Life isn't easy. I am here to remind you that our stressed-out society *needs* your music *and* your message. This is why choosing the names of your songs carefully is so important. People are looking for a *message* in the title of a song that sparks their curiosity, regardless of the music's genre. People are looking for a *solution* to life's problems. As a singer, songwriter or musician, you *provide* that solution to them.

How Naming Your Music Affects Sales

You'll recall earlier in the chapter, I mentioned how the naming of your piece can have a huge impact on sales. There is a very little-known strategy that applies, and the *dollar amount of your payments might be affected by your choice of name.* Therefore, I, again, encourage but not require you to choose or change the names of your songs very carefully.

To begin with, you must tell music fans something about your song before they hear it. You want to have a song title that has an encouraging message of some kind that might tempt die-hard music lovers to take the chance and stream your song, even if you are not included in their favorite genres. *You can do this within the song's title.* But there are *tricks* to doing this that you might not be using to maximize interest by music fans of other genres to listen to *your* song.

For example, if your chorus starts with the words, "Time, time, time" in an explosive manner, you might mistakenly name the song "Time." It's likely that *time* as the beginning of your chorus is a "sweet spot" that feels good to you as the artist. And your hope is that if it feels good to you, it will feel *great* for the music fan. The problem is that this tells a potential listener *nothing* about the song.

However, if the next word or section of the chorus is "I Promise You a Child," consider that there are millions of women and men, in our country alone, who are trying to have babies, but are having trouble conceiving. They are feeling depressed.

This is where you come in to help. You might be an up-tempo pop artist, while they prefer hard rock or heavy metal. But if they reach a station that has your song on it and it says "I Promise You a Child," people in pain as they try to have a baby but have had problems conceiving might sacrifice the 3.5 minutes to stream your song in an effort to cheer themselves up and give themselves some possible inspiration or *hope*. They will know that, at worst, if they sacrifice 3.5 minutes of streaming your song and it's not their favorite, they've wasted no significant time. Yet, you *still* get paid for the stream and the stream came from a die-hard, hard rock or heavy metal fan who would not otherwise even have *listened* to a pop song. They

6

might even enjoy it and want to keep hearing it in their collection. After all, musical tastes that are diverse are also, indeed, eclectic.

In this example, "I Promise You a Child" is part of the chorus—words you believe in—and it tells the listener something about the song, which might cheer someone up and entice them to stream it. You have helped them—and yourself as well by getting *paid* for the stream.

If you are an instrumentalist, you might not want to just pop up with the first word or image that comes to mind regarding a specific instrumental or album title. This is something we all have done. Instead, be creative and name the instrumental in a way that reaches out to a certain portion of people in the marketplace who could respond to that song name by listening to it. Thinking seriously about the mood of the instrumental and its style can give a partial helping hand, but you will still need to decide the best name that resonates with that mood and style as you think of a larger, open group of listeners who you might not have reached before.

You want a verbal title of the instrumental that creates a metaphorical, half-second "story introduction," that sparks the imagination of a potential fan's idea of what a wordless song might feel like. You want to pique their curiosity in what they'll hopefully feel in a song with no lyrics.

The greatest example I can think of regarding a truly amazing, heavy rock-and-roll instrumental and music video is Joe Satriani's "Summer Song." He thought about this name carefully. The result? It is *truly* a summer song and was a major hit that had no lyrics or words in the song. Who would not want to listen to a "Summer Song?" The title alone tells us so much about what Joe Satriani's song is about—or at least how we

7

might feel—and many will be tempted to listen to it only to love it, without even knowing beforehand whether it had lyrics or not! So, carefully consider your song title if you are an instrumentalist or singer-songwriter.

## Your Message in a Name

Now, let's say you are new to the music industry, and you write a brilliant hard rock or heavy metal guitar instrumental single or album and want to submit it to Spotify and other digital music providers. As an alternative to a name that resonates with the mood of your single or album, you might want to name the single or album with your name as the artist, followed by the type of music style or instrument you play in the song. As an example, there is nothing stopping you from titling your song, *"Your Name:* Hard Rock Guitar Instrumental" or *"Your Name:* Heavy Metal Guitar Instrumental," if this is your specific style and you are trying to get known to music fans. As a bonus, you will have titled your song with a musical style that is often entered into search engines by hungry music fans.

There is nothing wrong with giving your song a common name, even if it is the same as a frequent name for a musical style typed into the search engines. Your actual recording retains its integrity as long as that's your song's true genre. This not only helps music fans who search for these specific musical styles, for example, on Spotify, but you *may* stand a chance of showing up "higher" on Spotify for potential fans who will provide you with paid streams while the actual body of musical work contained in your musical product doesn't change.

Once again, I am not pushing you to alter your artistic vision, but I am suggesting that it's wiser from a keyword searchability and marketing standpoint to earn you more money for paid streams while not having to alter your *actual* material!

Remember, you can title your work by your type of music genre. No one has specific dibs on titling their work according to a specific genre! If you write piano ballads as either an instrumentalist, or a singer-songwriter who writes piano ballads with vocals, you can still call your album *Piano Ballads*, which can still encompass an entire album or single. If you are willing to do this then, once again, when a music fan searches for "piano ballads" or "piano ballad" in Spotify, you *may* rise up higher in their search. Or you can name an album *Pop Music* or *New Pop Music* for the sake of reaching Spotify users.

Other useful keyword phrases, which could also be used as album names are

- *Symphony Music*
- *Classical Symphony Music*
- *Hard Rock*
- *Heavy Metal*
- *New Hard Rock*
- *Opera*
- *New Opera*
- *Opera Singer*

The possibilities are endless. A sale is a sale, and your key goal is to *sell*.

In closing, every song-naming strategy I've mentioned above can be employed for all digital distribution channels, and for all your albums, EPs and singles. You need to see the naming of your songs in a whole new light, as opposed to creating a vague name for a song in just one second. You can choose a name that tells music enthusiasts something intriguing about what they are about to hear, to inspire them to click on the song and stream it. If you don't, you've missed an opportunity for a paid stream or repeated streams—often by the same person who is not normally into your genre.

I've shared this lesson with you so that you can create more sales of your music. After all, potential listeners might not be enticed at first to stream your song. Entice them with a great song title that, ideally, can speak to a person or a certain group of people. And use the specific musical style strategies, if you choose to, so that you can name your albums or a single according to what a Spotify fan specifically loves and will type into their search box. As always, the choices are yours. Whatever you decide to do, I say, "Go get 'em!"

# 2

## RECORDING AND MASTERING YOUR MUSIC

Now that you have named your single or album, you're ready to record it! You could record that tune playing in your head with a smartphone or tablet. Capture that idea quickly. You could even record a full album with these mobile devices. But for a professional product, you're likely to use a home studio. And after you record your music, you have a range of affordable services that can help you master your sound. This chapter will show you how to do both—professionally *and* affordably.

### Recording Your Music

A home studio can be budget-friendly, and consist of a computer with recording software, a 4-track, an inexpensive guitar, keyboard and microphone, or whatever you can afford. Your home studio is whatever you want to include in it, so you have a canvas for your musical masterpieces. Be *proud* of your home studio, no matter how simple or elaborate you make it. Most importantly, be proud of *yourself*. I know you can do this.

## Pro Tools by Avid Recording Software

Pro Tools by Avid is the world-renowned, leading industry standard of multi-track recording software for your music and vocals. Although it can be expensive for many of you on a tight budget, I have great news. There is a free version you can download directly from their website that might be enough to get you started. There are also paid options.

If you are adding just a few instruments and vocals, the free version might be all you need. This software will raise the bar in the quality of your recordings. This is why it is so preferred.

## Audacity Open-Source Recording Software

I have more great news for those of you on a tight budget. There is an open-source application called Audacity that can function as a *complete* recording studio for your computer. Unlike Pro Tools, you must record your instruments and vocals one at a time on each track; not at the same time. It will run on most computers. Search for it online and make sure you don't download a false copy of it. Your computer will usually warn you. As an open-source application, Audacity is *free* to use.

As we travel further into the development of your product as a single, an EP or an album, please realize that, just like the concept of a preloaded résumé template you might find on Microsoft Word, no one will ever know what methods or strategies you used to create your recorded musical masterpiece once it is done. In other words, they won't know what kind of recording studio equipment you used—expensive or budget-friendly. The average music fan will not question how you did the recording if they love it and it sounds professional, and just plain GOOD.

> ***Take Note:*** A musical track you think is a demo can
> be regarded as *finished* if it sounds *crisp and clean* and
> is well-packaged, even if it's done at home on a
> dinosaur computer using Audacity or just a 4-track.

People may try to talk you into using other expensive music
recording software because they think that Audacity is unprofessional or "cheap." They may feel they are looking out for
you, or they may have other personal reasons for trying to steer
you away from any recording option that isn't "the best." Often,
they just want you to know they are aware of the best so they
themselves can sound like they are ahead of you. Or, they just
might want to sound wealthier than you are.

It all comes down to the actual recording, though! You can
think of yourself as "smarter" and "more talented" than they
are, because you are producing an excellent recording for less
money. You do not need to purchase any expensive recording
software right now if you are not in a position to. It might be
provided for you one day if you procure a recording contract,
but for now, you have the free recording options just covered
here.

## Making the Most of Your Vocals

As an artist, you already know there are usually two key aspects
to a recording—*the music track* and *the vocals*, unless, of course,
if you are recording *just* an instrumental. When I first started
recording songs professionally and was no longer going to an
outside studio to record the music, I recorded all the music
myself in a home studio, and took the finished musical tracks to
a studio to record *just* the vocals there. I left it to an engineer to
mix my vocals. Overall, this is a great strategy you might want

to consider. It is a shrewd strategy, but not a must. Do what works for you. You are the artist. This is your vision. You are the one in control.

Another option is to ask an experienced musician friend whose recordings you like and who has experience with home recording, to record your vocals and mix them for you.

You *can* cut your own vocals, too, if you don't have a choice because of a tight budget. Just do your best to make sure you mix your vocals *well* and that the whole vocal recording has perfect pitch. Here are two key tips:

- While it might be easier said than done to record and mix your own vocals if you don't have experience doing this, just take your time and focus on blending your vocals well with the rest of your music, just as you normally do when recording just your instruments. Your voice is an instrument, so you may find that you are a natural at mixing your vocals with your music at home.
- You might want to add a *tiny* bit of reverb or treble to sweeten the way your vocals sonically blend with your music. After doing so, listen closely to those vocals on a good pair of headphones and make sure that you have not added too much. Listen to those vocals on a good set of speakers as well so you can compare how your vocals sound on headphones versus speakers. Think of the concept of adding a *tiny* bit of reverb or treble to your vocals as adding just a pinch of salt for a sumptuous dish. This can be done to make your vocals blend more, sonically, with the instruments. If you add more than a pinch, your vocals might have too

14

much of an echo, just as that gourmet dish might taste a bit too salty.

As your career grows, you will eventually be recording your music and vocals with an engineer at a professional studio. This is obviously the goal. If you can afford it, go ahead and record your music and vocals at a professional recording studio. Shop around for the best rates and try to negotiate an additional discount for a larger block of studio time, if possible. You know better than anyone else does what your own financial resources are and what you can and cannot afford to do.

Keep in mind that many artists make a *huge* critical error during the recording process when they use a professional recording studio and engineer. Due to the hefty cost of recording studio time, often the level of importance for their vocals gets downgraded. They focus ninety percent of their studio time on the music, taking only the final hour or so to do the vocals because they can't afford more time. This strategy is *very* unwise and, unfortunately, the most common of mistakes an artist can make. This leaves little or no time to develop those *sacred* vocals and vocal harmonies.

Your vocals, if you are a singer, are the most important part of the song. No matter how good your music is, a bad vocal track will wreck the song. It is good to know that you have the option of doing just the *musical portion* of your whole project, which we will now call your *product*, entirely for free at home in your home studio. You can then take out a large block of professional studio time with an engineer for recording just your vocals and blending them with the music you bring with you.

## The 4-Track Trap and the Solution

If you have a 4-track portable studio device that is analog, such as a vintage Tascam 414 PORTASTUDIO that records on cassette, plus a computer or laptop, you can record your music onto the 4-track recorder and bounce, or *ping pong*, your instruments back and forth, as you likely already know how to do, so that you can layer tracks infinitely.

But what if you find that you haven't *ping ponged* tracks correctly and have run out of available tracks/space to use from doubling up too many important lead instruments? You might be left with no tracks available to record your vocals or that all-important vocal harmony. Do not despair. Let me show you how to "rescue" your song.

Here is a trick I taught myself during a recording emergency I had at my old home studio many years ago:

1. Run a cord from the 4-track mixer into your computer or laptop's microphone jack.
2. Record the music into Audacity, and save the file in WAV format.
3. Record the entire production *back onto* your 4-track, but on a single track of the 4-track.

You've just created three or more tracks on your 4-track portable studio for additional instruments and vocal layering.

You can even take an old CD or cassette with a song you feel was unfinished or lacking significant vocal harmonies and, essentially, do the same thing:

1. Get a small, portable CD player and/or a cassette player.

2. Run a line from the headphone jack of the CD or cassette player into a single track on your 4-track portable studio. Now you have freed yourself up to *add* to your song.

3. Once you finish the song on your 4-track, run a line from your 4-track into the microphone jack of your laptop or computer, saving the file in Audacity as a WAV file.

4. From there, you can add stereo sound, additional effects, and burn a CD or save as an MP3 or WAV that sounds like a digital recording, even though it was previously reduced to analog.

No one will know how you accomplished this. Most people will not be able to tell that your recording started off as analog. The software on your computer will make it sound digital and atmospheric.

I developed the above tricks out of desperation years back, and I'm dedicated to sharing them, especially with artists who have great songs collecting dust on their shelves. So many artists think they didn't layer enough instruments, or they layered a vocal with an instrument on one track and ran out of any more tracks to use. They can't remove the principal vocal track from the unfinished recording, and they want to add more vocal harmonies. Years pass because the artists feel so down on themselves for making a recording mistake in the first place.

Oftentimes, they are struggling with the danger of being perfectionists, and they have actually wasted perfectly good songs when nobody hears any difference, except for the artist. Being a perfectionist can make someone abandon a project. Use my strategy above, and you are free to continue developing the song. No matter how long ago you wrote or recorded your song, it is *new* to the public if/when you finally choose to release it. You can bring your old, unfinished recorded songs back from the dead.

> ***Take Note:*** You may not know that The Beatles successfully recorded "Please Please Me" on a 2-track recording console. If they could do that, then with my advice above, you really have no excuse for not recording your music *now*. Your sound will be even more developed than the primitive 2-track technology, as your work will take on a digital and stereo sound with a little manipulation within Audacity. When you've completed the strategy for bringing your song(s) back to life, remember to save all your music as WAV files for future use, which you can also convert into MP3s, both using Audacity.

## Mastering Your Finished Songs Has Never Been Easier or Cheaper

When your song is finished, but not yet mastered, you are in what is called the *post-production phase*. Mastering your music is the final step to complete your audio/song recording. *Mastering* is the process of balancing out all of the sonic elements from every sound in your recording. It takes the sounds that should sound a bit higher and makes them higher. It takes the sounds that should sound lower and makes them lower. A bass or rhythm section that sounds too buried and soft can often be brought to the proper audible level, bringing the beat and the bass to your desired pulsating level.

A great mastering job will often reduce or eliminate any unnecessary atmospheric noises, such as a hiss or any other sounds of excess "air" that might hinder the quality of your precious recording. Most importantly, mastering optimizes your recording so that everything done during the process to improve your song sounds great, with all the sonic adjustments remaining intact and sounding the same across *all* different music/media formats that your song is played on.

Take advantage of the super-amazing new breed of online instant mastering companies. The paid online mastering programs are very inexpensive compared to the days when you had to seek out a qualified engineer and work with them, hour by hour, and usually in-person. Advancing technology and innovation within the music industry has made mastering available for you whenever you are ready to take a further step in the quality of your music so you can market it, sell it, get industry attention and be *proud* of yourself.

Two well-known companies offering mastering services are:

- **Landr.com** offers a *free,* instant mastering tool for MP3 songs. Additionally, there is a very affordable cost if you upload a WAV file instead. With this said, even their basic free MP3 mastering offers a *significant* level of improvement to the overall body and fullness of a song.
- **CapitolStudios.com**, based at the Capitol Records building in Hollywood, CA, now has mastering services available online. Plus, Capitol still has the roster of expert engineers attending to your project back from the days before their online service.

You might want to experiment with the free, online mastering services for an MP3 first. Get familiar with the before and after results that you can hear on your laptop computer speakers or headphones. Afterwards, you can move up and spend a very modest amount of money for a full-blown mastering job using a WAV file that you will upload instead of an MP3.

With a company like Landr.com, the whole process takes just minutes. You can follow the progress of your job online and Landr.com will email the finished track to you. With other online mastering companies, it might take a set amount of days. This just means that the work is often gone over by hand by a skilled engineer who tweaks your sound waves on a computer screen. This is a *very* good thing.

Whatever you choose to do, not being able to master a project is *not* enough of an excuse for not releasing your music.

> ***Take Note***: One thing you should really take great care with if you are planning to record a full-length album, EP or anything with more than one song on the same product, is to make sure that the volume levels to *all* the songs are even with one another. Think of the pause that takes place between the end of one of your songs and the beginning of your next song if the two are released on the same product. You don't want the next song, or previous song, to sound like it is at a different volume level, and make listeners adjust their own volume up or down on their stereo. It will not sound high-quality, and it won't sound like a body of work that is truly cohesive. Instead, it will sound amateurish, as though you took a few songs and threw them together just to create a quick but low-quality EP. When all the levels of the songs are even with one

another, your music will take on the feeling of a complete production where the songs truly belong together in the specific order of songs that you chose to include.

Again, all the levels to all the songs must be even within a body of work. If you are a vocalist, your vocals must be as close to perfect as you can get them. Do the best that you can, keeping in mind that there is no such thing as true perfection. Not all vocalists are created equal. And remember what I said earlier about adding an effect, such as reverb or treble.

If you have an engineer set the levels for you, then bring in your finished tracks to an engineer at a recording studio. Although many studios offer mastering packages that can be expensive, many also offer the service of just evening out the levels to your songs, to bring your album's levels to pristine quality, at a reasonable cost. Discmakers.com offers this type of service, in addition to full-blown mastering. This is also a great thing.

Whichever process is right for you, you now have information to record your songs and to make an informed decision on how or if you want to master your project.

For those of you who have not yet recorded your songs, don't fret. Everyone works at their own pace. In my professional experience over the years working with successful individuals, I see that the wisest of them already seem to know not to distract themselves by comparing their progress to the progress of anybody else. You can *always* start by recording just a single to get your feet wet, so you have something ready to launch before you continue reading. Of course, do not let that stop you from creating an album or EP if you're eager and *ready to go*. I do advise that you get, at the very least, a single prepared before continuing to read. I *know* you can do it. I will patiently await your return and see you in the next sections and chapters.

Voila!

Take the time to congratulate yourself. At this point, you need to protect your music by copyrighting your work before you distribute your music to Apple Music, Spotify, and other digital outlets, or make CDs available for purchase. The next chapter tells you how to protect what you've worked so hard on.

# 3

# PROTECTING YOUR MUSIC— COPYRIGHTS AND PUBLISHING RIGHTS

I cannot emphasize enough how vital it is that you copyright your music *before* you make your music available for sale. Below, I will take you step-by-step through the process of *safely* copyrighting your music so that your precious work is protected. Once you copyright your work and have it distributed on all the major distribution channels (covered in Part 2 of this book), your music will be ready to place on your website and announced on social media (covered in Part 3 of this book).

## Registering Your Copyright Online

Based on my extensive research and experience in copyrighting everything from music to film over the years, I am going to teach you how to do this for your music in the *simplest* and *correct* way. We are going to copyright your music online at the U.S. Copyright Office by having you upload your finished MP3(s) as a single, EP or album in a way that makes you pay only *one* fee— regardless of the quantity of songs.

1. Go online and visit eco.copyright.gov to get started. (If you ever have any questions for the Copyright Office, you can call them at 202-303-7000 in Washington, D.C., Monday through Friday, 8:30 a.m. to 5 p.m., Eastern Standard Time, EST, except federal holidays).

2. In the upper-left corner area of the **Home** page, there are blank boxes for an existing user's **User ID** and **Password**. If you are not already registered, select the link that states **If you are a new user, click here to register.**

3. Register for a free account to create your Electronic Copyright Office Account online.

4. Once you are registered, please see the next section for the correct online form to fill out.

*Take Note:* Once you complete the steps below, it will take several weeks for you to receive in your actual mailbox your paper certificate/proof of copyrighting your work. But you will be issued an instant receipt in the meantime as proof that you have initiated the process. This instant receipt is one of the real beauties of copyrighting your music online—in addition to the reduced cost of doing so.

Form SR—SR Stands for Sound Recording

Your music is a Sound Recording, so choose **Form SR** out of the list of choices. The reality is that filling out Form SR is the *most* important, and generally the *only* form you need to fill out once you have created your online Electronic Copyright Account.

Whether you are a singer, songwriter or musician, the form will ask you questions about whether anyone else can claim Copyright Status or Partial Ownership of your work. If you are the only one who wrote, recorded and performed your songs, then the answers are "No." If someone else wrote half the song, recorded and performed with you, make sure you answer "Yes" and name *all* parties involved in the songs.

Answering the question about my level of contribution was always a nightmare to me when I got started, and it stumps many artists to this day. We worry we might explain too much, explain too little, or we simply don't know how to answer such an important question in a precise way. It took lots of trial-and-error on my part, until I finally aligned with an expert who told me the most succinct, complete and ethical way to cover *all* areas of the precious music you worked so hard on.

When asked about your specific contribution to a work, simply answer "Words, Music, Performance." That's all. If you have other artists who also contributed all those three parts to your song and you've *ethically* credited them as parties on the form, you will use the same answer.

If you are a songwriter who writes the words and music, but doesn't usually perform, you might want to record your voice and sing the song anyway for the purposes of a complete and honest copyright, so that you can also include "Performance," as your contribution to the song. The Copyright Office is not in the business of judging your vocals!

If down the road, you agree that another artist will perform your song, you can resubmit your material online as a *changed version*. This holds true for all singers, songwriters and musicians who change or redo a song to sell to the public. It can always be registered online again as *a changed version* of the original.

> ***Take Note:*** If you only intend to release a single, but have a pile of other finished or unfinished songs recorded, bundle them together and upload them on a single Form SR so that you don't have to pay multiple fees.

## Form PA—PA Stands for Performing Arts

Form PA, for Performing Arts, is a form that many major labels or established talents fill out and pay the additional fee for when they release a single, EP or album. You might choose to fill out this form as well and pay the fee. You are perfectly free not to. Here is the reasoning I was taught for when Form PA is not needed, and when it's important to complete.

*Form PA Not Needed*—If you already took proper credit on Form SR by including the word "Performance," this makes what you wrote on Form SR tough to argue against.

*Form PA Is Important*—The true purpose of Form PA is generally for copyrighting a film or anything related to the performing arts. Technically, this can mean a nonvisual performance—a sound recording. But if you've already completed form SR for your recording, you should be covered. However, if you have produced a full-scale music video—which I not only show you in-depth how to do in a future chapter, but also how to possibly make money from—you should also file a separate Form PA and pay the fee, even though you've completed Form SR. If you make a music video and fill in the area that asks for the parts you contributed to, make sure to include the phrase "Performance and Sound Recording" within your contributions. If you have any concerns when filling out any section, you can ask the United States Copyright Office.

## Music Publishing Rights

When you registered your copyright, you established your *music publishing rights*. These are the ownership rights to your own song. If you wrote the song and recorded all the music and vocals entirely yourself, you own one hundred percent of your publishing rights. The percentage of your ownership of your *own* song is critical and determines how much you will be paid for sales, streaming and licensing. An unscrupulous individual who thinks your song might be a hit could attempt to trick you into selling your song to them for *one* flat fee, which is also usually a *very* low fee. Do not ever sell even one percent of your music publishing rights. If you do, that person will own a percent of the song you wrote, just as if they wrote it themselves. Keep the full one hundred percent of your publishing rights if you wrote it yourself!

If you wrote the song with another person and published it, each of you would own fifty percent of the publishing rights to the song, or a different percentage if you have contractually agreed otherwise, and you would split your earnings based on the contracted percentages. If you look back to the lesson on copyrighting your material, you have already reported your percentage of rights to your song(s) to the U.S. Copyright Office. If you sell your rights, these copyrights will be voided and another party could own them and likely copyright them.

I do not want you to be tricked into having even one percent of your publishing rights taken away from you by any unscrupulous companies through deceptive language written in their contracts. One company tried to do this with one of my songs, but *disguised* it as a record contract. I recognized their tactic and refused. (See the Appendix for an example of a bad contract and a good one).

This company was trying to "purchase" my song, as if they wrote it themselves. Later, the song they attempted to buy from me, and which I refused to sell, became featured in a movie. If I had sold all my publishing rights to that unscrupulous company, I would never have gotten the song into the movie. It would, instead, now belong to a bunch of crooks who would have gotten away with one hundred percent of the publishing rights to the song. Yes, these types of entities exist! They are looking out for themselves first and often have language in their contracts that is meant to trick you, or even trick an inexperienced attorney out of your ownership so they can profit from your work.

A good attorney, especially one with experience working with legal aspects of the music industry, will not be deceived by virtually *any* type of music contract. All contracts usually contain a compromise for both parties. Contracts can be rewritten or have clauses marked out or added in from either party. Yes, you can alter things you are not happy with and it's best to have a competent attorney help you in this process. If you are presented with a record contract and it is with a legitimate company, either major or independent, you should be able to keep *all* your publishing rights.

***Take Note:*** Two vital warnings:

- With a legitimate record contract, the company will *never* ask you to pay anything.
- With a legitimate record contract, the company will *never* ask you to give up ownership of your original

song if it is in its original form and you wrote 100% of the song and have proof of copyright. If you work with a producer or co-write/alter a song with the label that you originally wrote yourself, you might have to negotiate ownership levels if it becomes a new or altered song.

## Legal Assistance

If you need assistance protecting your rights—now or in the future, if you receive a contract proposal as one example—visit one of the legal sites listed below and ask them to refer you to an entertainment attorney or small business attorney who is capable of addressing copyright issues or reviewing the contract.

> **Take Note:** The incredible Songwritersguild.com also offers assistance and can get you the advice you need on music contracts you receive. This is just one of the many reasons to research their website and consider joining SGA.

If you receive a contract, you will have the attorney review the offer, explain any parts of the contract you'd like, and tell you if the contract is appropriate and safe. Do not sign *anything* you don't understand. Below are three organizations that can help:

- **Avvo.com**—Here you can ask anonymous and free legal questions on the message board and get a huge amount of responses from attorneys. On this site, other attorneys will often vote on each other's response to your question for accuracy in the answer. You might choose a lawyer based on their responses and legal specialties. The bottom line is that you want your document reviewed. Your attorney can help you propose any changes that might be needed within the contract. Then, you can sign when all is correct. This also shows the record label that you *have* an attorney.

- **Calawyersforthearts.org**—Another option for legal assistance is the website of the California Lawyers for the Arts organization. This is a cost-effective resource to tap into since this resource deals exclusively with protecting the rights of the artist. If you live outside California, you might still contact them to find out if they can help you, or refer you to a similar organization in your state.

- **Legalshield.com**—You must be very careful when it comes to understanding the details of the types of contracts you might eventually, and *hopefully*, be entering into. Legalshield.com is a monthly, prepaid legal service offering unlimited document reviews, phone calls and other options. They list small businesses as the closest match to what you are: a small business. I suggest you consider contacting them and finding out if they can provide you with the type of attorney you need for music contract reviewing. You might find them a useful, affordable legal service for document reviews and other areas of your life.

# II

---

# THE BUSINESS OF MUSIC

# 4

# PRODUCT FORMATS AND HOW THEY COUNT TOWARD SALES

The music industry is rapidly shifting toward a completely digital marketplace, which is greatly convenient and has opened many doorways for you to sell music. Music fans love that they can get an entire album downloaded *instantly* as soon as they make their payment online. They also love that they can listen to a large selection of music through streaming services without purchasing individual songs or albums.

In this marketplace, which product formats should you choose for your music and what should you consider when making that decision? First, it's important for you to understand how the music industry tracks the sales of digital and physical music products, as the methods may influence your production choices. Second, I will cover the various ways you can format your product.

## Understand the Importance of Music Tracking

Beginning several years ago, the Recording Industry Association of America (RIAA) started to include music products offered via streaming services as part of the equation to determine if a full album can still go Gold (500,000 U.S. sales), Platinum (1,000,000 U.S. sales), or Multi-Platinum (2,000,000 U.S. sales made plus any additional sales of 1,000,000 for that album in the U.S.). It also made the change to provide the music industry with a broader understanding of what artists and songs are being streamed or sold digitally online. This is good news because subscribers to streaming services alone are often not purchasing individual songs or albums.

The RIAA made the decision to include streaming because these services are so much on the rise, versus the often-declining sales of singles and albums. Please, do not let this stop you from recording a single or album for distribution. Artists are still creating singles and albums and always will because they must in order to get ingested into the streaming services and be part of the tracking system!

In this new music industry, you, as a new and aspiring artist, get tracked in the same way as the major label artists. Nielsen SoundScan, owned by Billboard magazine, is the official, electronic tracker of music streams, online digital sales and CD sales. They track and record sales of singles and full-length albums. This is a great thing because it doesn't matter what your work environment or resources happen to be. The more effort you put into promoting your online music, the more your music will be tracked if it streams, sells as a digital download, or is an album on a physical disc. The same tracking rules apply for new, unsigned artists and established artists. Your sales will automatically be tracked, and the sales figures will show up in the accounting section of your distributor. We will discuss distribution in Chapter 7.

### Definitions of Digital Singles, EPs and Albums

Before we get into the details of how Nielsen SoundScan goes about tracking sales, I'll review definitions of three common music products.

**Single**—A single is, simply enough, a single song you choose to release. Yes, it *can* be just one, single song you release.

**Album**—The term full-length album, in today's new music industry, is the same, in one respect, as it always has been, just in different formats—a CD or a digital, instant download version of the entire album for music fans to purchase.

**EP**—*EP* is an acronym that stands for an Extended Play recording. I personally have loved EPs ever since I was a kid. EPs can best be described as mini-albums that contain an average of four songs.

For example, a highly coveted artist with a hard-to-find song might release an EP featuring four songs:

- The title song of the EP
- A song from their previous album
- Two remixes of the featured song

If you are considering releasing a single and have a few more songs, but not enough for a full-length album, you can now see the advantage of taking three or four songs and creating an EP. Since you can set the price of your EP lower than a ten-song album, you might substantially increase your chances of selling the whole EP instead of just one song on it. Additionally, you can point out to fans that if they buy an EP instead of 3 or 4 singles, they get a better value for their money.

## How Digital Download Sales Are Counted in Nielsen SoundScan

How physical sales and digital streams and sales are tracked by Nielsen SoundScan can be confusing and often change in varying degrees. Below, I have summarized the process that has taken place in our recent times.

If you release a single:

- Each sale of your single song will be tracked by SoundScan as a sale of your single.
- Every 10 sales of your single song will count as 10 sales of your single song, and 1 full album sale (10 sales of a single song is equivalent to one album sale, even if you haven't released an album).
- The music industry can see your sales figures. You will also be paid and have proof within your online distribution account that you have sold.
- If you want to market yourself to major music companies that have not had a chance to notice you and your music, here is an example. If you have 20,000 in sales, that is no small feat, and you have serious leverage. Many companies might seek you out with sales even less than this amount.
- SoundScan will also track and allow the music industry to see that in this example, you have sold what they consider to be 2,000 albums—your 20,000 singles divided by 10. This puts you on the road

toward the prospect of going Gold or Platinum in the future. But you will have to make a lot more sales to see that happen. What's most important is that, today, you are given a chance. Your sales are tracked exactly the same as already established, famous artists.

If you release an album:

- If you release an album online for digital download and a music fan purchases the entire album at once as a full body of work, you will be tracked by SoundScan for the sale of 1 full album.
- You will be paid for the sale of 1 full album.
- If music fans buy only some songs from the album as single downloads, you will still be tracked and paid for each song music fans purchase individually.
- For every 10 purchases of songs from the album as single downloads, you will still get tracked as having sold your full album.
- You would get the same music industry visibility and sales for a song off your album as for selling a single. When you sell your full album, you have the added advantage of an album sale all at once as opposed to selling 10 of one or more of the songs over time.

*Take Note:* If you have recorded a 10-song album and strongly feel that 1 or 2 of those songs are hits, you can and perhaps should put more promotion efforts into those one or two songs. Again, if ten music customers buy a specific single song online, you are tracked as having made one full album sale.

## Music Streaming vs Downloading a Single Song: How You Get Paid

In the case of customers who stream a song of yours instead of buying it outright, Nielsen SoundScan tracks every 150 streams as a single paid download. If a music fan decides to purchase and download that one song outright, you will be tracked and paid for a single paid download immediately. The purpose of this system—150 streams equals 1 paid download— is to ensure that you get tracked and paid for that sale of your single even if people are possibly streaming your music for free on different platforms.

You might be asking whether you get paid for an individual stream. The answer is "sometimes," but it is very little. To compensate, you want as many streams as you can get, and, of course, you ultimately want listeners to purchase the single as a direct download, outright.

It's an ongoing possibility that Nielsen SoundScan might change these formulas in the future, but the same formulas have been generally accurate for several years.

## Choosing a Product Format

Given what you've just learned about how Nielsen SoundScan tracks streams and sales, this may influence which format(s) you choose for your music. In fact, the choice of format for your music product is determined by many aspects, from the decision whether to go digital or physical to how many tracks you might want to include in an album. Luckily, in today's music industry, you often don't have to make a choice. You can produce both CDs and digital files, and distribute them economically. You can simultaneously put your physical CD up for sale online and have your digital music accepted, digitally processed, and ingested (included) by all the major online music retailers: Apple Music, Google Play Music and Spotify.

## CDs

As a music product, CDs will always be relevant to some degree, I hope. There is always a music fan that prefers a CD with album art and packaging. Die-hard music fans often want the CD version to add to their collection of music in their homes. CDs often let them feel more connected to their favorite artists. Additionally, CD players are usually in most modern automobiles with no word yet on whether they will stop being included. But you cannot deny the appeal of digital formats for easier sales and for streaming services.

## MP3, WAV and Other Digital Formats

As you know, there are several dominant digital formats for downloadable music, with MP3 being the most common. Broadly speaking, they can be divided into formats that compress the music and formats that do not. MP3, MP3PRO and AAC compress the music to make the file smaller with some loss in audio quality. Formats such as WAV and AIFF do not compress the music and is favored by demanding audiophiles.

Many companies recommend you provide your music in WAV format for ingestion into the digital music download marketplace for its higher quality sound.

## Full-Length Albums

In today's music industry, a full-length album—physical or digital—should consist of no more than 10 songs, since 10 songs is the established number for what constitutes a full album for digital download. The reason for choosing not to release more than 10 songs on your album has to do with the sales of your CD and *not* your digital sales and streams.

If you sell an album on CD with 12 songs, you will only get credit for 1 album sale. Another artist who sells a 10-song album as a digital download online will also be credited with 1 album sale even though their album had fewer songs than yours. Do not cheat yourself by putting more than 10 songs on your album if you plan to release the same album digitally. Most artists do not know this, including some legendary ones who do not understand the new tracking model.

> ***Take Note:*** By sticking to the maximum of 10 songs per album, you won't have to worry about competing with artists who offer fewer songs but get the same album credit. At the same time, you will not earn less if you add more songs to your album than the recommended number of 10 songs.

## EP—Extended Play

While your EP can be placed on a CD with a title and cover, it might be wiser to consider doing just a digital release since it is not a full album. It will be ingested into the major digital music download and streaming services while, most importantly, providing online listeners more musical choices of your work.

The same rules apply for EPs as for albums when it comes to Nielsen SoundScan's electronic sales counter. Sell 10 songs as downloads and they are reported as a full-album sale. Get 1,500 paid streams on Spotify, Apple Music, or any other streaming format where music fans choose to listen to the song but not download or "own" it, and you will be tracked and credited for an album sale.

## Ringtones

You have them on your phone already, maybe from your own favorite artists. Why not offer your music in ringtone format? It is easy to make ringtones from your own music so people can buy them for their phones. Visit a website like SnipSell.com to learn more.

# 5

## CREATE YOUR MUSIC COMPANY

### Create a Company

You are a singular talent! You are a singer, songwriter, musician, and no one can duplicate your talent. You are unique and individual. So what I say next may sound conventional, and therefore contradictory to your individuality, but...to build your career, one of the most important things is that you must start and build a *company*. I emphasize this not only because I want you to be successful financially and gain the visibility you deserve, but it is also great for your self-esteem.

The reality is that this is your very own small business you are creating. I want this to excite you and motivate you. If you just want to release a song as a single, you may feel no need to start a company or to follow the advice that follows. That's okay. You don't have to. However, please read on so you learn that, should you change your mind, creating your own company is far less daunting than you think, and will set you up for future growth.

## What Kind of Company to Be

The kind of company you start reflects what you want to do in music. You might want to start a *production company*, which means you will sell your own musical products. Or you might want to start your own *independent record label*, which means you will sell not only your own products, but possibly other artists' work *if* you choose to. To begin with, it's a good idea to focus on your own work, so it's wiser to start with a production company. In the future, you might *need* or *want* to grow your career by signing with a larger record label, and larger record labels might be interested in your production company down the road.

Whatever direction you choose, the idea is that your company will serve as a professional platform to present your CD, your digital music, your act (if you play live) and all other products related to your music that you want to sell.

## Naming Your Company

Being the creative person you are, you may already have a name in mind for your company. There is a simple way to find out whether or not the name you want is already being used by someone else: Visit the United States Patent and Trademark Office online. Please understand that at this stage it's not necessary to patent your company name or a logo. Right now, you are simply looking to see if the name you love most is legally safe to use.

Following are the steps to confirm that your desired name is available, and then to officially name your company:

1. Visit the United States Patent and Trademark Office

online at uspto.gov. You can go ahead and do that now, so you can actually see the screens as we go through the steps involved.

2. At the top of the **Home** page are several tabs. Click on **Trademarks**. A list of choices will appear.

3. Under the section that reads **Application process**, click **Searching trademarks**.

4. This will take you to the page titled **Search trademark database**.

5. On this page, you will find the Trademark Electronic Search System, known as *TESS*.

6. Click on the bar that says **Search our trademark database (TESS)**.

7. In the **Selection Search** option box, click on **Basic Word Mark Search (New User)**. This option states that it cannot be used to search for design work. This is okay. We are not interested in searching for trademarked design work; we are interested in searching and obtaining your desired company name.

8. You will be taken to the page where you can enter a search term for your desired company name. The radio buttons for **Live and Dead** and, separately, **Plural or Singular**, should already be selected. We are most interested in finding out if the name you want is "Live" or "Dead."

9. Fill in the first name you want to use for your company in the **Search Term** box and click the **Enter** or **Return** key on your computer.

10. If the name comes up as **Dead** or **Abandoned**, then Congratulations! You can use the name.

11. If the name comes up in your search as **Live**, then

you cannot use the name. The site will also provide you with information on the company that is using the name. *Take Note:* Although it is best to stay clear of a name that another company is using, depending on what city or state you live in, you might be able to use the same name if you are in a different industry. With this said, it is safest to stay clear of the same name that another company is using for any purpose.

12. If the name you want is already **Live** and being used by another company, hit the back button and insert your second, third, etc. choice(s) of names you want to use for your company until you get a **Dead** or **Abandoned** result.

13. If you get a message on any of these searches that says **No TESS records were found to match the criteria of your query**, just hit the back button on your computer and click the **Contact Us** link at the top of the screen to email the USPTO and check on the availability of the name you want to use. Ask them if the name you chose is okay to use.

14. Once you have learned that you can use the name that you want for your company by receiving a **Dead**, **Abandoned**, or **No such record in database** message, you should be all set to use the name. Hooray for you!

## Make Your Company Name Official

As you now have received your valuable "clearance" to use the name you desire, it's time to officially register your company name at your local city government offices. Completing the first two steps below will make you an official company. The final two steps will get you set up with your company mailing address and a professional business logo.

## Step 1: Get Your Business License

You will need to apply for a business license. There are licenses for different types of businesses—called *entities*—such as Sole Proprietor or Corporation. The entity you choose, in part, determines how you will be taxed on income, and the fees you will be required to pay. Since you are just starting out, for now, I suggest you choose the entity designation of an Individual or Sole Proprietor.

## Step 2: Announce Your DBA

The business license is issued in the name of your company. If your company name is anything other than your actual name, you will need to file a DBA, which stands for "doing business as." Even though you have conducted a USPTO search and found your desired company name is available, you are also required to let the public know you intend to use this name. It gives the public a period of time to declare if someone is already using it. Because your USPTO search showed that your desired name is available, it is generally unlikely another company will come forward to say they are using the same DBA. Still, the process is required to make your name official.

Once you obtain your license, you will be provided with a list of newspapers or other publications in your area that you'll need to contact so that they may publicly announce your DBA. The local newspaper (usually for a small fee) publishes the name of your company and your intent to use it.

The general laws require that this small, often classified-size newspaper ad must be published for a certain number of weeks. Oftentimes, the minimum time required by the laws in your local city, town or state for keeping a DBA ad in the newspaper is one to four weeks, but it can vary depending on where you live. Your local business license office will tell you the required amount of time your DBA needs to run in the newspaper. Once that time has passed and no one has claimed preexisting or current use of the name, you are in the clear.

## Step 3: Obtain a Company Address and Phone Number

If your home is your current studio or office, you will want to obtain a separate mailing address for your company—one that is not a PO Box. You may use your own home address if you wish, but there are benefits to having a separate mailing address.

An office address/private mail address that is different from your residence looks much more professional and, above all, protects your privacy. The business mailing address is simply for receiving or sending mail and packages for your company. You can rent a "business mailbox" from a company such as The UPS Store® (different from the standard UPS shipping company). To find similar companies near you, simply do an online search for the phrase "business mailbox" plus your city and zip code. These companies provide you with an actual street address, which will look more professional in the eyes of the music industry and media.

> *Take Note:* If you grow into a corporation, law requires you have a company street address. A PO Box is not acceptable, so you might as well get your private PO Box now.

47

For the same reasons, you may want a phone number that is separate from your home number. If your home phone number and voicemail are the same as your business phone number or you use your cell phone exclusively, make sure you always answer the phone professionally and that the welcome message on your voicemail reflects your business.

Your callers don't need to know that you run your business out of your home. If the television is on or the vacuum cleaner is running when a call comes in, turn off any and all of these things before answering the phone. And when you answer, even if you're out of breath because you're in the middle of exercising, you should still sound like a producer or executive who has been calmly working in the studio or at a desk.

Are you not sure what to say when the phone rings? A great strategy is to answer by simply saying, "Production," and nothing else.

### Step 4: Create Your Logo

The final step I cover in this chapter is the fun part! You'll need a logo for your new company. There are logos that look like they cost $2,000 to produce, for which people paid $50. There are also logos that look like they cost $50 but have a $2,000 price tag. Out of a universe of options, I am listing three examples for help to either have a winning logo premade, or create one yourself, almost instantly:

- **AAA-Logo.com**—I've used this, and it is a very inexpensive piece of logo-creation software that you can download. You can instantly create a winning logo for your company using an almost endless choice of templates within the application. Have fun with designing your logo and choose the look and colors you love most.

- **The Logo Creator**, by Laughing Bird Software—Available for Mac, Windows, and also as an app for your smartphone.
- **Logo Maker**—A highly rated app for your smartphone that allows you to create a professional logo at no cost.

If you want to check out other logo apps, search online for "logo maker" and you will get *thousands* of additional suggestions!

Remember in our earlier discussion about the United States Patent and Trademark Office, we were not interested in looking to see if a design had been trademarked? When creating/designing your logo, the worst-case (and least likely) scenario this early in your career is that a company comes along and says, "We already have a trademark or patent on that logo design." It is almost impossible to think you will ever be approached by another company with this concern, but if that were to happen, you can either completely change or slightly alter the design.

The silver lining if you did have to change your logo is that your company will have a new, fresh look and will appear to have grown and evolved. Given the convenience of these logo software/app programs, you might decide down the road that you want to change your logo anyway.

Congratulations on creating your new Music Company! It is possible that it took you only one to four weeks to complete this amazing milestone in your creative and professional life. Perhaps it took you a little longer than this. If it did take you longer, that's okay. Work at your own pace!

# 6

## SET UP YOUR PROFESSIONAL MUSIC WEBSITE

In this digital age, to achieve your goals as a *professional artist,* you absolutely *must* have a professional music website. Your website will be the main, online portal for music fans of the new company you just created. In the beginning, it will be the *only* place where people can go to purchase your music from your new company. You will be using it not only to sell your music, but also to sell music-related merchandise such as T-shirts and mugs, to post information about your live shows if you perform live, and to communicate with your listeners and fans.

This chapter provides a blueprint for building an actual store on your computer. Building your social media presence is also key, and we will cover social media pages and how to set them up after we build your website. In Part 3, we will discuss much more about social media and multiple other ways of promotion.

## Choosing Your Website Host, Address and Design

If you are on a tight budget but want a professional-looking website design, there are many do-it-yourself website companies that specialize in designs for singers, songwriters and musicians. Read on.

### Website Host

I recommend any of these four website hosting companies. The first three are do-it-yourself sites that are designed specifically for music artists and the music industry:

- Bandzoogle.com
- Hostbaby.com
- ReverbNation.com
- Wix.com

These are additional highly rated choices with plentiful hosting and design options:

- A2Hosting.com
- BlueHost.com
- GreenGeeks.com
- HostGator.com
- Hostinger.com
- InMotion.com
- iPage.com
- SiteGround.com
- StableHost.com
- WebHostingHub.com

If you want to do your own further research, as new and innovative hosting companies for musical talent are always showing up, a quick online search will find more. The above-mentioned website hosting providers are currently rated the highest, and all have been around for quite a while.

Your basic e-commerce—the mechanics for buying, selling, pricing and collecting money—will be provided for free by the website host. Service fees from financial institutions behind your e-commerce will apply, depending on your setup. With do-it-yourself website hosting, everything, including sound files, can be published instantly online from your home computer, which makes otherwise costly updates completely free. The do-it-yourself approach will enable you to update your own site with little or no experience. If you want to share a simple update with your fans regarding new music, a live show, or news regarding your career, you will find that it is much easier to do this yourself on one of the selected website platforms.

## URL/Website Address

Upon signing up with a hosting company, you can choose your URL/website address. Choose your name as the singer, songwriter, musician, or production company name you might have chosen for the main part of the URL. For example, *Your-OwnName*.com.

## Website Design

As mentioned, you can easily design your website at one of the suggested hosts without the need to pay a designer. The host companies provide plenty of premade designs that you can personalize and are great for all of your musical needs.

Kindly keep in mind that if you decide to hire a professional designer down the road and "move" your website from a do-it-yourself hosting service, you may not be able to move the actual site if the existing design software and hosting are all in *one*, and the hosting company owns all of the designs, preexisting photos and templates. In such a case, you might have to rebuild your website.

On the positive side, with a do-it-yourself website, you can always save all your text and pictures onto a USB flash drive, CD-ROM, and most importantly, in the "cloud" of your choice. This allows you to have all of your essential elements saved and accessible should you choose to completely redesign your site in the future or move to a new host. You should carefully save all of your creative files, regardless, using the above saving options, so you do not lose any of your precious, original work.

### For an Exceptional Personal Photograph, You've Got Options

An important piece to include on your website is a photograph of yourself. You don't need to look like a supermodel, but it's important that your photograph look professional, and that it highlights who you are and what you and your music stand for. A bad first impression can be likened to packaging an anniversary diamond ring in a brown paper lunch bag. With all the hard work you put into your songs and music, you want to take every opportunity for potential visitors of your site to want to take the next step—*listen* to your music. A good photo can prompt visitors to want to learn more.

In this digital age of professional, media-quality photography—available even on most smartphones—we are all better photographers. Well, some of us are. If you're not, you have options.

At this point, there is no need to hire an expensive photographer to capture the personal magic that is your unique look. Maybe you have a friend who is a good photographer. Or you know a photographer you can strike a trade deal with. There might be an eager photography student in the local college who can capture your magic while building their own portfolio. Photography schools combined with photography students usually have the best equipment, training and creative ideas.

Whether you are your photographer or someone else is—your photograph must look *professional*. This is not a hard task at all. A few key tips:

- Make sure the photograph is clear and sharp.
- A 72dpi or 96dpi photograph is perfect to use on your website.
- A 300–350dpi photograph is necessary for print media, a CD cover, posters, etc.

Take your time to create the perfect photograph that does not look like a selfie, and make sure it is in full high-definition if you're using your smartphone. You want the photograph to look polished. Most importantly, you want to always *feel* polished. You are the real deal! *You get the picture.*

You will be using this photo in many ways, so no matter which avenue you decide on, download these three FREE app "goodies" from Adobe Photoshop to your smartphone. They allow you to enhance, color, crop and do everything you need to polish your photo without *any* experience using Photoshop whatsoever:

- Adobe Photoshop Express

- Adobe Photoshop Lightroom
- Adobe Photoshop Mix

## You're Ready

Now that you have your website design, address, your logo and an amazing photograph, you are ready to spread the word to the world!

# III

---

# MARKETING YOUR MUSIC PRODUCT(S)

# 7

## ADDING SOCIAL MEDIA TO YOUR WEBSITE

As the main online portal for your fans, your website should also include links to social media to promote your music. In trying to decide which social media to use, a great place to start is to think of two or three of the top-selling, most relevant and famous music artists, then visit *their* professional music websites to find which social media companies and social media links they are using.

The huge number of social media companies out there is staggering. And it's vital that you keep your posts current. The idea of keeping all of your social media pages updated can seem daunting. The good news is that not only does Instagram duplicate your posts to other social media sites if you allow it to in your Instagram settings, but it is perfectly okay to copy and paste all your current posts and photos to *all* social media companies you choose to work with. Famous musical artists have everything duplicated onto all of their social media pages.

Many times, the do-it-yourself websites will provide ready-made links to duplicate your posts to other social media. Other companies might not. Take a look at the following list of social media platforms. Pay particular attention to the last one in the list, Addthis.com. Regardless of whether your web hosting company provides premade social media links, Addthis.com not only provides social media links for free but also provides tools to market your online presence for free.

Here are the major social media platforms that famous, big-selling musical artists are choosing to use and link to from their own professional music websites:

- Facebook

  **Take Note:** Do *not* use a personal profile as the principle way of spreading and selling your music on Facebook. This is a mistake that so many artists make. While you can and should let your friends and associates know about your latest projects on your personal profile if you have one, you *must also* create a *professional* Facebook page to sell your music. You will use your professional page to promote to the public. Facebook pages are designed for business, they have a specific page preformatted for musicians and artists, and it protects your privacy from the masses of potential fans who you don't personally know. When you register on Facebook, you can create a professional page even if you do not have a personal profile.

- Instagram
- Twitter
- YouTube
- Addthis.com—the amazing online company that will not only provide you with all the social media buttons

you need to place on your site, free of charge, but will also provide tools to help promote your online presence, free of charge.

Installing a **Share** button on your website is very important. Any fan who visits your site and finds the **Share** button can share your material through their email, text or onto their own social media site(s), regardless of which social media sites(s) your fans happen to prefer.

Addthis.com has so many social media buttons to choose from that some of them may or may not be needed for you to post if you do not have all those social media accounts of your own, or choose not to have one or more of them. The list included above may be all you need for now. Addthis is so diverse that Facebook, Twitter, Slack, Reddit, Pinterest and many others are available as options to include on your website through Addthis.com.

Choose the most popular social media sites mentioned above to start. You can expand later. Our goal for now is to cover the most popular social media sites.

> *Take Note:* **Email Stays Important!** When thinking about social media, absolutely do not forget about email lists. Email remains one of the best ways to create and maintain a personal connection with your fans to build sales and loyalty. Mailchimp.com has an excellent, free email marketing platform. They also offer more advanced, paid options as you grow your career.

# 8

# SPOTIFY AND DISTRIBUTING YOUR MUSIC TO THE MASSES

Congratulations on all your *hard* work. Now, I will show you how to distribute your music in the simplest ways possible.

## Invest Your Time in Spotify

Every singer, songwriter and musician asks how they can make money on Spotify. To fully answer this, I must first correct some misconceptions you likely have heard about how to do this. You may have heard or read that you can't make money in the music industry anymore. Don't believe it and don't let it stop you from your dream. You are at a huge advantage as an aspiring singer, songwriter, musician or any type of musical talent right now. Streaming services are the most crucial avenue for building actual sales.

What's even better is that almost all the streaming services are connected now. When you go for distribution, which I will show you later in this chapter, when you follow the distributor's simple requirements for ingestion of your music, you generally *automatically* get ingested into all the major streaming services at once, including Spotify.

Think of one of your songs as a single $10 bill you invest into the (metaphorical) Spotify "Stock Market" (I literally only mean their streaming service), and you earn significant money over time if you name your work correctly, as we discussed in Chapter 1, and *do* the work. Unlike the real stock market, where you often "buy, hold, and wait," you have more control with your Spotify "investment."

## Stations, Stations and More Stations

You can—and should—be doing a lot of work trying to get on as many stations on Spotify as you can. Okay, but how do you do that? Ahh...read on. It is a great strategy to start by creating your own station and to stream your own music. But the beauty of Spotify is that it operates through a unique streaming model. The company decided to allow die-hard music fans the opportunity to "get involved" by supporting the artists and songs they love and creating their own stations. There are countless numbers of "individual stations" set up by businesses or fans across many areas of the world. Those stations share songs with listeners and with other stations.

Having your music shared by so many stations increases the potential to significantly multiply your earnings. But it can take some time. You must be very patient and you must persevere to the best of your abilities. Not all stations are created equal. One station might be small and have simply been created by a fan, receiving little or no attention. Another station could be a cash cow if you are able to get your music onto it. Spotify has released a plethora of instructional videos that can help you become successful. If you follow the upcoming tips, you may find that as you grow your visibility on smaller stations, the larger stations will be more likely to find your music and add it to theirs.

In addition, the quantity of smaller stations still matters as they can help sell your music product. Selling any type of inexpensive product or stream requires selling a huge amount of *product volume*—the number of song(s) you sell or stream.

Music lovers feel important on Spotify because they are involved in sharing and discovering music. They help music fans *find* your music. This is the key takeaway in understanding Spotify and how it has the potential to make you money. If any station decides to add you to their rotation, you should thank them and be a support to them. It could lead to friendship, an ally in music, or both. But that's not all.

> ***Take Note***: You have the option of releasing a single, an EP or entire album directly through Spotify without having to choose a distributor at all. You can sign up directly through Spotify and get your feet wet exclusively with them if you do not want to choose distribution at this time. Some of you might want to start by releasing just a single through Spotify and focusing on the success of that until you get some promising results. With this said, you can always choose to just take advantage of mass distribution, which I cover in the next section, if you choose to. You are in control.

## Distribution Companies—CD Baby and TuneCore

I am focusing on two major music distribution companies—CD Baby and TuneCore—that highly established artists used when they were first starting out...before they "made it big." But even major artists use TuneCore for ease and simplicity within this new and changing music industry.

There are other distribution companies out there, so you have choices, but these two pioneers have been around for a *very* long time and offer everything in one place. I am covering them below and what they offer for distribution options to save you time and a lot of research.

Distribution companies are very advanced today and they offer so many services, that an artist can easily feel that all they need to do is sign up for all of the options, sit back and let the distribution companies handle all the promotion. Nothing can be further from the truth.

You *must* do your own marketing and promotion, which will be covered throughout this part of the book. No one will do it for you. You cannot sit back and think that things will automatically happen if you sign up for the right distribution program with all the bells and whistles. The very distribution companies would give you the same advice, and they offer free training on their websites.

It's up to you to entice the masses to make use of the distribution network—to actually listen to and buy your music.

## CD Baby

CD Baby has been around for decades. It has grown to become a one-stop, full-service CD and digital music distribution company that now offers everything an artist might need in one place—starting from scratch—for getting your music out there and available to the masses. CD Baby offers distribution to over 15,000 record stores and 150+ digital music distributor outlets around the globe!

"Sell and Stream Your Music Everywhere" is their main tagline. "Global music distribution. Get paid weekly. No annual fees." is their supplemental statement. Not having to pay an annual fee to keep your music ingested in all the digital distribution networks is *extremely* important. Some other music distributors require at least a yearly fee. Kudos to CD Baby for not doing this and *never* having done this in the history of their company.

Let's take a look at several of the services that CD Baby offers.

### Distribution

Rightfully boasting more than 150+ global music distributors, with more being added all the time, the best known of CD Baby's partnered paid download and paid streaming sites include Spotify, iTunes, Apple Music, Amazon and YouTube (as you will learn *a lot* about in the next chapter about music videos).

### Partnerships

CD Baby has a separate Income Stream Program they've developed through partnerships with YouTube, along with Google Play, Pandora, iHeartRadio and many of the other major digital music sites. You can easily search on the CD Baby site for all of the new partnership programs available by entering the names of the companies that have income stream programs. There are new ones developing all the time. This means more income potential for you.

## *CD Production*

Although you might be tempted to—or have been advised to—produce a high volume of CDs, I recommend that you only press 50 CDs with graphics to get you started. CD Baby offers full CD manufacturing *with* graphics in packages starting out at just 50 CDs. I don't want you to have any unnecessary overhead.

You will be assigned a barcode for your CD through CD Baby. A barcode is that white sticker with black lines and a code number that is on every product in existence that you buy from a store. The difference here is that *your* barcode will be encoded to work with Nielsen SoundScan, mentioned previously. Your barcode is specific to your music album so the number of your sales can be tracked.

> *Take Note:* Also, since you want to get credit for
> *every* sale you make, including at all live shows at
> venues that work with Nielsen SoundScan, you can get
> credit for your performances *and* albums sold through
> Nielsen SoundScan's Venue Verification program. And
> remember, you will also get tracked/credited for all
> your paid streams and digital downloads through
> Nielsen SoundScan. CD Baby provides you with all
> Trending and Analytics Statistics to keep track of your
> sales and paid streams so you know how you're
> progressing.

When considering your CD design and what to include on your packaging, if you choose to release a CD instead of only a digital release, be sure you include *all* credits, and the names of all songs on the CD inside and back sleeve(s). Include typed lyrics if you choose to, but most important is that list of all musical content. Above all, especially in terms of cutting down costs, there is nothing better than an album that is *lean and mean* in design with a well-crafted visual design. You can use that photograph of yourself you worked so hard on as the CD cover if you prefer, or another image. The visual design can be simple, as long as it looks professional.

And remember, you must display your professional music website address on your CD, in the sleeve and on the back of the traycard insert that shows on the back of the CD case. You want consumers and fans to know where they can purchase your music, join your mailing list, buy tickets for your shows if you perform live, and of course, purchase more of your CDs and digital downloads, which is *most* important. Additionally, in the sleeve and on the back traycard, list links to all paid streaming music platforms you have listed on your professional music website, which gives visitors a choice of streaming services.

If you don't put your professional music website address on your CD, it is a *major* mistake and lost opportunity. I don't want this to happen to you! Make sure it is on the back side of the CD case and listed prominently so that a consumer can see where to buy the CD online at your professional music website, even at a later time! You might earn the huge majority of your music royalties online, but if your fans remember your website address, they might buy more music later. CD manufacturing companies can add the logos of any social media sites you have joined directly on the back of your CD as well.

### *Cover Song Licensing*

CD Baby also offers easy Cover Song Licensing (once, the hardest type of licensing to obtain). If you cover another artist's song(s), CD Baby will provide full mechanical licensing and *management* of royalties you might owe for each of your sales of a cover song. Basically, you can freely record a cover song of a well-established artist *first*, then simply upload the song to CD Baby to obtain a license to use the cover song. Whatever royalties you owe the original artist who wrote the song will be tracked for you. CD Baby explains the process in more detail on their website, as well as the advantages of recording cover songs.

CD Baby currently takes a 9% cut for any digital sale. Amazon.com will also sell your vinyl records through CD Baby, in addition to all other musical formats mentioned. CD Baby has a warehouse that can hold copies of your CD and, when one sells, they ship it to the customer and keep $4.00 of the sale.

Don't worry, the fees are standard in the industry. A lot of the major digital distribution or streaming companies also charge their fans monthly fees to stream your music. They also take a percentage when someone purchases a song or album of yours as a digital download. This is how all these companies can afford to stay in business and keep you in business. All these companies reveal what fee they keep when you make a digital music sale.

If you decide to only pursue a digital release with CD Baby instead of a CD, you can always create download cards to take with you and sell at your live shows. Visit Bandcamp.com or ProCards.com for more information. A download card is roughly the size of a credit card. You can sell them to fans at the price you choose. Ten dollars is a reasonable price, but feel free to set your own price. It is very convenient and prevents you from having to carry bulk CDs with you to your live shows. You might even decide to hold a contest or raffle during your live shows, giving one or more download cards away for free to a lucky audience member.

## TuneCore

TuneCore also offers digital distribution to over 150 digital distribution companies, including Spotify and all the other major companies, such as iTunes, Apple Music, Amazon— companies you have heard of plus many others you might not have heard of. They boast that they do this in over 200 countries and territories and, overall, this is a huge feat.

Furthermore, you get to keep every single penny—a full 100% of profits from your digital sales and paid streams. This is *great*. TuneCore mainly distributes your music in digital format. However, you have the opportunity of releasing a CD-R, which is manufactured only on demand, through TuneCore's arrangement with Amazon on Demand. The CD-R is manufactured only when there is an order for it. This is fantastic because it truly means that you do not have to carry any CD overhead stock at all.

Many years ago, as digital music became mainstream, I remember very specific, high-profile, and well-established musical talent were suddenly switching their distribution methods to TuneCore. It took me a bit of time to realize that these artists were ahead of the changing trend. TuneCore has a phrase on their website that states, "There are no barriers to your career." This is my philosophy in this day and age within the new music industry. I couldn't agree with them more.

Just keep in mind that, unlike CD Baby, TuneCore charges a yearly fee for their distribution services. While I would feel remiss not to point this out, TuneCore *does* offer just about everything that CD Baby has to offer in terms of distribution services and coverage of royalties and territories. They also provide you with e-commerce for your distributed music. The major advantage of TuneCore—and what may justify the fee— is the advantage of the artist retaining 100% of the sales. With this said, some artists think that the yearly fees charged in order to provide this advantage can really add up. Other artists have no issue with the yearly fee. It is your decision. You are in control.

> ***Take Note:*** You really should research both companies and see which services or packages suit you best. As in everything in life, always read the fine print. Digital distribution is forever progressing, and these companies often change distribution packages to offer you more visibility.

## How to Place Your Music on Your Website

At last, you are ready to place your music on your professional music website that you built! You hopefully understand the importance of copyrighting your music first. Manufacturing and distributing your CD should happen only *after* copyrighting your music. Making the wise choice of not placing your music on your professional music website until after you copyrighted it is an admirable testament to your patience and seriousness as an artist.

The process of placing your new single, EP or album on your website could *not* possibly be simpler.

*Take Note:* Please understand that a distribution company sales page is NOT to be used IN PLACE OF your professional music website. Having the sales page alone is looked at by the music industry as unprofessional and a sign of an undeveloped talent.

Whether you use CD Baby, TuneCore or some other distribution company, you might get a *sales page* that comes with the distribution package you choose with them. If you do get a sales page, it is this sales page that you will link to on your professional music website. We are going to cover these steps in this section.

You should include your photo or album cover and the 150 to 300-word biography from your professional music website on this special sales page first. You can choose your own prices you want to sell your music for. They will show you how to do so.

Once you have chosen a distributor for your music:

1.  Take the assigned address of the sales page if you are provided with one, and place that link on your own professional music website. If you are not provided with a sales page, simply move on to the next step.
2.  In the weeks that follow, as your music gets ingested into Spotify, iTunes, Apple Music, Amazon, iHeartRadio, Pandora and all the other 150+ digital music sites, go to those major sites and look yourself up on them. Copy the links from several of the major online digital distributors of your choice, and paste the links on your professional music website to give fans and consumers choices for where to stream or purchase your music.

***Take Note:*** Some online streaming radio stations do not pay artists at this time since listeners are not choosing the songs that are streamed. I am just pointing this out so you are aware of it. You should not be concerned about it because all artists are in the same boat and the rules might change. Just make sure you focus on displaying regular streaming and sales sites that are not radio and that *do* pay.

## 9

## EARN MONEY WITH A MUSIC VIDEO
## AND YOUTUBE

In this digital age, the music industry continues to change in ways that give you more access and opportunities for professional growth. This is a truly wonderful time for making your musical dreams come true. You *deserve* it.

YouTube is one of those opportunities, and a major platform for promoting your music. It is the *number one search engine* used by the masses to find music, particularly *new* music. Even if your music is not new or is in a little-known genre, you can become just as successful if you follow my advice in this chapter. There is always a niche of listeners for you on YouTube. You have probably already heard of a few "stars" that made it by developing successful and well-optimized YouTube Channels.

**Take Note:** Some startling statistics about YouTube:

- YouTube is the world's second largest search engine and second most visited site after Google.

74

- YouTube is the second most popular social media platform, with 1.9 billion users.
- 500 hours of video are uploaded to YouTube every minute.

In addition to the visibility you receive on YouTube, you can also take advantage of a Partnership Program that earns you revenue for streams of your music video. A sync-licensing arrangement that CD Baby has created in partnership with Rumblefish is also in place and connected to YouTube. Through this partnership, the music from your music video is given electronic access to film and TV music supervisors, with additional access to producers of video games, commercials and more. YouTube also has its own monetization program for videos, so if you get enough subscribers, it can mean even more potential income.

TuneCore has a similar program established with YouTube. What this means is that you can get paid for the use of your music on YouTube in multiple ways. Finally, YouTube has even newer programs available now for music fans. These carry monthly membership fees for the fans.

### The Style, Format and Production of Your Music Video

There are three key components for creating a successful music video:

- Filming
- Storyline
- Editing

Your music video-shooting options are immense and diverse. You are in a time where you can create a music video masterpiece on a very limited budget. Here are some options you can use to show how truly great you are.

### Filming

Here are two low-budget suggestions that can still net high-quality results:

- A Samsung smartphone, an iPhone or any other brand smartphone that can film in Full High Definition (FHD), 1920 x 1080, is perfect for creating your music video. Your smartphone can be placed on any inexpensive tripod with a universal adaptor that adjusts to all smartphone screen sizes. iPhones have been used to shoot entire motion pictures and streaming TV shows, as well as other types of smartphones.
- Or you might want to visit a local college that has a Film or Broadcasting program, seek out the head of the department, and present what kind of help you're looking for. Most students are looking to build their own careers in production, which often begins with the making of music videos. Through the college, you might find a student who can arrange a multi-camera shoot on higher end equipment. You will have a polished music video, and the student will gain valuable experience for their résumé and portfolio.

Along with the filming requirements, there are two other *key* elements for your music video—that *great storyline* and *editing*.

## The Storyline

As a singer-songwriter myself, who has also made award-winning short films with the use of my own music, I am inspired by a time in the past when a music video had a great storyline, or at least a *meaningful* one. Back in the days when music videos went mainstream, thanks to MTV, talented singers, songwriters and musicians had wonderful opportunities to work with talented film directors and create true, mini-musical films with genuine artistic merit. From an industry point-of-view, these music video masterpieces served as commercials, so to speak, to sell the musical product/song. This approach hasn't changed, and it works.

If you can write your own storyline for your music video, that's fantastic. If not, as mentioned earlier, see if a qualified friend or family member can help, or if you can trade your musical talent for a script from a writer.

## Editing

The added secret to any successful music video with a storyline is the editing of the visual content. Great editing can take a low-budget project and make it look very expensive. Professional editing is expensive and is often a huge factor in what ultimately makes a film expensive to make. However, a student might do this for free and *enjoy* it. Ask the student what editing software they use at their college. They will be using the very latest.

If you want to try your own music video editing, the basic movie editing software that comes on a MacBook can do an amazing job while making sure your music is perfectly aligned with your edited visuals. For Windows users, even Microsoft

Movie Maker, which comes on some versions of Windows, can accomplish the same task. If you have Windows 10 as your current operating system, you can download Movie Maker 10 for free at the Microsoft website, or by simply doing an online search for Microsoft Movie Maker, which will take you to the specific download page at Microsoft.

The first company mentioned below offers convenient and often inexpensive video production equipment rentals. The second company also offers full-scale production services where they will create your music video for you:

- **Budgetvideo.com**—If you want to make your music video with a storyline yourself and you or your friends have professional film or digital film experience, this company has top-of-the-line camera equipment that they can rent and ship to you inexpensively, regardless of where you live.
- **Productionhub.com**—This is an online portal of creative media talent services that lists filmmakers with equipment who will shoot and design your music video for you.

Venues for Your Music Video

If your music video is ready for the world to see, that's fantastic! The beauty of creating a music video with a genuine storyline is that, from your home computer, you can access a number of venues for showing your work—from film festivals to YouTube.

There are online platforms where you can upload your music video, add your biography and submit your professional music video with a storyline to thousands of film festivals. These film festivals are in the United States, Canada and all around the world. I have been very successful with numerous awards and screenings using this method.

Here are two preferred online film festival platforms for you to choose from:

- FilmFreeway.com
- festhome.com

You should only choose one of the two so that you don't end up submitting a movie to the same festival twice, which would make you look very unprofessional. Plus, if you stick to just one of these platforms, you will be able to fine-tune your platform and build a portfolio that stands the test of time. Using only one platform is also easier and simpler to manage. They each submit to the same number of festivals.

## YouTube

You can easily set up a YouTube account and use this extremely popular platform to promote your music. Here are the key steps to follow—and suggestions for building and communicating to your list of fans and subscribers:

**Create and upload your page photo**—YouTube requires you to upload a photo, especially if you want an amazing-looking page.

Use a panoramic photo that is 970 pixels in width to upload in the blank area of your new YouTube page. Make sure the photo looks cool and crisp and is filled with life and scenery. There is a no-tolerance rule for any unoriginal work, including photos. Your smartphone can easily convert your photo into a panoramic photo, as can the three, free Photoshop apps for your smartphone that were shared in chapter 6 on setting up your professional music website. Here are the three, free Photoshop apps for your smartphone, as a reminder:

- Adobe Photoshop Express
- Adobe Photoshop Lightroom
- Adobe Photoshop Mix

Add your professional artist photo or company logo if you wish on your YouTube page; they will appear in front of your panoramic photo.

Choose a great, professional-looking background from YouTube that, most importantly, matches the color scheme of the panoramic photo and image you chose for your artist photo or logo.

**Upload your video**—Next, go to the upload section of YouTube's main page and upload your music video, regardless of whether yours has a storyline, you used just still photography or original artwork, showed yourself performing live, or created a mini Artist Documentary.

**Choose your keywords and keyword phrases**—After you've uploaded your music video, go into the Settings section and fill out all required keywords and descriptions for your video. Fill in your full professional artist name in the keywords section, your musical style and everything you can think of relating to your musical style.

As an example, if you are a heavy metal guitarist, you can and should get very creative with keywords, i.e.:

- heavy metal
- heavy metal guitar song

- heavy metal artist
- heavy metal artists
- electric guitar
- hard rock
- hard rock guitar
- guitar
- guitar music
- new heavy metal
- new heavy metal song
- heavy metal songs

Make sure that you separate each keyword or keyword phrase with a comma. Click **Save**. The more keywords and keyword phrases you come up with, the better the chances of people finding you. You can also cross-promote with other artists of the same or similar style by choosing keywords and keyword phrases that relate to both you and other artists.

**Write your descriptions**—Once you have saved your keywords, in the Description area, it's a good idea to write a 700-word description that includes all of your keywords and keyword phrases. You might consider writing separate 700-word-description essays for each of your songs, telling their story, and incorporating appropriate keywords and keyword phrases.

If you just can't seem to come up with these 700-word essays, write a few paragraphs, including your keywords and keyword phrases in them. Do the best that you can, and don't bite off more than you can chew. If you get stuck, stop, take a break, and come back to your writing, and add as much as you can. A good description will greatly increase the chances of your music being discovered. Many YouTube users are building and optimizing pages for their non-music-related businesses, which sell very expensive products. However, you are selling music and, because it is inexpensive as a one-time purchase, you have to sell a lot of volume to make all of this financially worthwhile.

**Set up your channel**—You need to set up your very own, customized YouTube channel to take advantage of the music monetization, even if you only have one music video. The idea here is that your YouTube channel creates and grows your brand for your name as a singer, songwriter or musician, much like the professional music website you already built. You can also create multiple channels, but for now, let's just focus on your own single YouTube Music channel. Fans can then subscribe to your customized channel and you'll be eligible for YouTube's music monetization programs. Simply choose **Create Channel** and follow the prompts.

Here are some great additional tools to highlight and promote your channel:

- YouTube will allow you to create a Custom URL (website) address for your channel that features your name or act. Your YouTube URL will look like this: http://www.youtube/*nameyouchoose*. Once you choose your custom URL address with YouTube, you cannot change it, so choose your name wisely. Make sure it's the URL name/address you want and, if possible, the same one you use on your professional music website.

- If the name you want for your YouTube URL is already taken, so the name can't exactly match your professional music website, make sure you choose a YouTube URL name that is very close to your professional music website URL name, or a name you have chosen to use as an artist. If you keep the names to both URLs as similar as possible to one another, hopefully the search engines will pull everything about you to the top of the first page of any search site.

- You can add annotations to the content of your channels, i.e., links to buy your music from the professional music website you built, as well as notes, thought bubbles on your music, etc.—but not too many. We don't want to put too many of these "word graphics" on your videos to the point where viewers might get distracted or dizzy. However, as you will see, if used sparingly, annotations are a plus in earning revenue—the prime goal if you want to have a successful career as a music artist on YouTube. You might also start making a nice income stream doing what you already love. If you earn revenue, it means you must be getting a solid number of fans.
- When you create your channel, you can create a playlist of your chosen songs, using your chosen visual theme. Your music videos can be set to play like a shuffled television version of a station.

**Benefit from the features of the Comments section** —You should use the Comments section to develop relationships with your fans. Be sure to ask questions in the Comments section of your channel. Start a discussion. You have the advantage of adjusting your Settings within YouTube so any comment posted by a fan must be approved by you first before the comment gets posted. This helps avoid any verbal abuse or inappropriate language from users who aren't really your fans or want to make you look bad. If someone leaves positive comments or questions, always respond. You can make potential fans feel important, as they should feel. Plus, you are just beginning your career so you should make it a virtue to answer and respond to every comment or question. Fans love to feel loved, important and connected in some way to their favorite musical artists. I want that favorite artist to be you.

**Communicate with your fans in the Comments section**—You can also communicate relevant information about your music, news and activities to subscribers by using your Comments section. You'll use it by informing subscribers about new music, interviews, concerts, etc. You will also encourage them to keep following your channel. You should do this about every two weeks, or at least every three to four weeks. Try not to wait more than a month.

> ***Take Note:*** While YouTube also enables you to disable incoming comments as protection from cyber-bullying or abuse, you really should let your true fans engage with you. As mentioned in Step 6 above, YouTube thankfully makes this possible by enabling you to preapprove comments before you allow them to post. Use this option, as it was designed to keep you safe while helping you to succeed and giving your true fans a voice!

**Use the YouTube Creator Studio to help you grow**— The YouTube Creator Studio helps you create higher quality video presentations and provides so many different options and features to help you engage with new fans and grow your online visibility within YouTube. The YouTube Creator Studio is also now available as a mobile app for your smartphone! Check out creatoracademy.youtube.com to see the full power you have at your fingertips, thanks to all of the resources YouTube has put together for you.

I want to reiterate that if you are consistent in maintaining your YouTube page and channel regularly, there is no reason to think that you won't *grow*. Consistency and gentle self-discipline create growth in most *any* endeavor one chooses. *You* are no exception to this.

## Alternatives to Music Videos

If you're not quite ready to make a full music video yet, you have some great options for creating other visual content. Here are several ideas to get your imagination—and actions—flowing:

- Live footage of your music is always a great option for YouTube, and YouTube has free animation tools for your music.
- If you don't want to make a music video with a storyline just yet, you might want to consider creating an interview—behind-the-scenes commentary of your music, telling people about yourself by showing off your daily habits, instruments and gear. You can create a mini Artist Documentary. You are only limited by your imagination. Songwriters, this is a *great* option for you because you can talk about yourself with your music playing in the background. You can even recite some lyrics or align with a singer to perform them.
- You might want to shoot a simple live performance of a song or a series of songs indoors, outdoors or with an interesting background, even if you have no audience. Just film it *close-up*.
- If not a full-fledged music video, consider a video

where your music plays over a still image or several still images. You can display your lyrics and promotional text such as your website address and contact information. This simpler form will allow you to create a presence on platforms such as YouTube. A lot of the time, people who search for music on YouTube are only interested in hearing the *song* anyway. Using a still photo, your song and lyrics give you visibility, even if it is not considered a complete music video.

- You might want to encourage people to do cover versions of your songs. This has worked for major artists. Even at this stage in your career, some people will redo yours as well, if you reach out to other artists and *ask* them to.

***Take Note:*** CD Baby's and TuneCore's arrangement with YouTube and other media companies mentioned earlier in this chapter will automatically gain revenue for you if another artist or fan "shares" your music video on their own YouTube channel, or posts their own video of your song on YouTube. This is because your song will be encoded when you join either CD Baby's or TuneCore's program, in addition to YouTube's own monetization program.

As you can see, you have many options to show off your talent. You owe it to yourself. Take a breath, close your eyes, and give yourself a moment to take this all in.

# 10

# SOME WORDS ABOUT RECORD POOLS

For those of you who are unfamiliar with what a record pool is, let me explain. *Record pools* are services that collect music from artists like you, and also from record labels. Record pools then distribute your music to venue DJs, who often subscribe to a record pool in order to cost-effectively get their hands on the newest music as well as add to their catalogs.

> ***Take Note:*** You do not have to be signed to a record label to be included in a record pool collection.

Obviously, there is the potential to get exposure for your music, especially when you consider that certain DJs and other professionals who subscribe to the pool might also have contacts that could be beneficial to you. Traditionally, record pools require the artist or record label to supply them with music in the form of records or CDs, though usually records. Think of the popular, but often underground *old school* genre, here. With the lucky advent of digital music distribution, some record pools offer artists and record labels the ability to get their music to a multitude of DJs via digital music delivery systems.

Exposure like this only has the potential to do good things, which is why I encourage you to research various record pools. Record pools are most advantageous for dance music, with or without vocals, and are good for spinning at clubs. However, you may be able to locate record pools for other genres that spin in other types of public environments, such as bars, restaurant parties or department stores.

Please keep in mind that it costs money to supply a record pool with actual records, and the cost might not justify the means, unless of course you have a smash-hit song you are performing live, or if an influential DJ takes notice of the value of your music.

There might not be as much, or any cost, if they accept digital files of a few of your songs. Joining a record pool is not something that will always equate to sales, but if you are an artist looking for exposure in clubs, it may be a fantastic way to network if you can continuously supply the DJs with your songs and get your poster and professional music website address on the walls of some clubs. What you really need to do is *perform live* in the clubs. Network with the DJs by going to visit them at the clubs. Not unlike the prospect of getting a prospective employer's attention, use the polite and patient approach and you might get the DJ's attention, along with the gig(s).

If you want to find the latest record pools, do an online search for "record pools." And if you want to make vinyl records—to submit to record pools or for other uses—do an online search for the best company and prices.

***Take Note:*** When looking for new companies to work with, read and listen to people you trust for recommendations and check out their record of business performance with the Better Business Bureau at bbb.org.

# 11

# CREATE YOUR ELECTRONIC PRESS KIT (EPK)

You have come so far and I'm incredibly proud of you. You've already taken valuable steps to get your music uploaded and distributed. Now let's cover another vital way to let everyone know about you and what you've created. We'll do this by creating your Electronic Press Kit (EPK).

Your EPK is an online, electronic résumé that shows off your very best music and overall image. It can be blasted out to multiple music industry personnel at a time and is a less expensive and *profoundly* more convenient invention that replaces the traditional, bulky black folder holding a paper press kit. It streamlines the process of promoting your precious musical work.

The company I recommend you use to create your EPK is Sonicbids.com. They have been around since the very beginning of the EPK and is arguably the one company that brought the EPK into mainstream awareness for musical talent. In addition to offering a world-class EPK format for artists, they hold endless numbers of contests with major music industry companies where you can submit your EPK for consideration by these companies. Additionally, Sonicbids has a business model that helps you network with other artists from virtually anywhere. They also give you the ability to book your own gigs if you perform live. You *must* have an EPK if you want exposure and greatly increased opportunities for success with your music. There are also many other EPK companies to choose from these days, and a Google search will reveal many. With this said, let's create your EPK!

1. Go to Sonicbids.com, or any music EPK site of your choice, and create an account.
2. Choose very carefully which song or songs you want to upload. Many listeners will only have time to hear the first song you've listed, so make sure that you put your very best musical material at the top and take the time to consider your second or third best songs, placing them in order beneath your first-listed song. Obviously, you want all of your material to stand out as professionally as possible, so if you think a song isn't quite up to par, then leave it out.
3. Make sure your photo and any artwork, including your album cover, are of the highest quality for uploading to your EPK. Sonicbids recommends that you have a 300 dpi (the standard quality used for photographs), high-resolution version of your photo and artwork in case media wants to reproduce it on paper. They also recommend having 72 dpi, low-resolution images for uploading, at a minimum of 600 pixels wide. While 72 dpi is not suitable for printing, due to low resolution, it is the mainstream format for images on the web in all industries, because they take up less space and allow websites to load faster.

4. You want to include a biography that is engaging enough for a music journalist to want to share your information. You can start by copying and pasting your biography from your professional music website to your EPK. As you accomplish more in your music, you will update your biography, adding new highlights and accomplishments.

5. As I stated earlier, having a meaningful music video with a storyline will attract the interest of venues and music journalists. If you have a music video of a solid live performance that shows you at your best, then make sure you upload it as part of your EPK. You want to create a multimedia presentation for the industry at large. *Take Note:* Regardless of whether you are a singer, songwriter or musician, if you do not perform live, or don't have a music video, then just leave those out of your EPK for now and you can always add them later.

6. Make sure you include a link to your professional music website.

7. Include an email address, designated for media inquiries.

8. Make sure your EPK package doesn't appear gaudy or complicated in any way.

9. *Never* make statements about yourself that could come off as self-serving—in your biography or anywhere else in your EPK. Let media professionals compliment you in a review.

10. Keep your EPK simple but tasteful in design, since media professionals and clubs will not have the time to go through every nook and cranny of your EPK. Be unique and engaging, but also be straightforward and to the point.

The fact that Sonicbids is able to connect a songwriter with so many other artists is all the more reason a songwriter should have an EPK. If you network with artists who sing, it might not only be considered an honor for an artist you reach out to on the platform to sing your song, but that artist might be a lot more established, and enable you to meet many *more* singers for your work as well.

Even if an artist is a lot more established than you are, you can still engage in cross-promotion with them and give something back. You might even make a friend, collaborator or close ally in your music career.

## 12

---

# YOUR LIVE SHOW (OR LACK THEREOF)

Even if you do not play live, or are not *currently* playing live, please do *not* skip this valuable chapter. After reading it, you might find that the strategies contained here will *inspire* you to start playing live. Read on and you'll see what I mean. With this said, the choice to play live is entirely yours and you can still have a successful music career without live shows.

If you *are* playing live, I strongly recommend you play out at clubs a *minimum* of once a month. Playing live only once a month might serve you well because you leave prospective fans "wanting more." Playing live only once a month can also make things easier on you, giving you more time to focus on your other promotional tasks and making *more* music to *sell*. Plus, you have more time to create an even better performance! Playing live once a month, consistently, will keep you safely in practice and "in the game." With this said, if you choose to play every one or two weeks and you can't resist performing, then *do* it. Just kindly keep in mind the advice I've shared in this paragraph.

For those of you who play live, use a calendar section on your professional music website and in your EPK, to list your shows in advance, as well as to sell tickets online and at the venue. ThunderTix.com is one company that enables you to sell tickets to your shows from your professional music website. Search for other companies that provide this service to compare prices.

Finally, if you want to perform live concerts online from your home, studio, or other venue, you must check out Crowdcast. Crowdcast.io lets you create free shows, meetings, seminars and so much more. As a musical talent, you can put on a concert in real time. You can invite all your fans from your email list and host concerts with a live, interactive message board. There are so many other features to this wonderful online, live video portal. You should be communicating with your audience, speaking to them about your music and encouraging them to buy it. You can offer a free show, arrange donations for tickets based on what people can afford as they watch from home on their computers, or you can set ticket prices. You can also save your shows.

## Take Over the Club on Open Mic Nights

Do not sell short the concept of doing some Open Mic Nights at clubs, especially with the tips I am about to share. You have a variety of options to find Open Mic Nights near you:

- **OpenMic.us** not only has a database for the United States, but also for many countries around the world.
- **Openmikes.org** is another online database that gives you all the Open Mic Nights across the United States. You just type in your city or zip code and you will get a listing of venues, distance to the venues,

their contact information and phone number, as well as the dates and times of their Open Mic Nights (usually once a week).

I recommend also calling the venues to make sure the Open Mic Night dates and times listed on their websites have not changed.

> **Take Note:** If you send your EPK to a venue that is not far from you, and you don't hear back, it is always better to just go and introduce yourself in person. Be polished when you do. Oftentimes, you have not had your EPK rejected by the venue. They just might not have had a chance to view it yet. When you introduce yourself to the booking agent, gently advise them that they have your EPK. If you are asked to send another one, send it right from your smartphone in their presence, showing them that it is absolutely your pleasure to send them another one. They might look at it and/or book you right on the spot to save themselves time. Plus, you look like the kind of person who doesn't waste time.

Oftentimes, you will only have to play *one* Open Mic Night to prove to a venue that you can perform well if you follow these insider tips—all of which apply for *any* live performance:

- When you get on stage, and it's your turn to sing your *single* song to an uninformed crowd and club owner, make sure you *nail* the song and really hit it out of the park. You can ensure this powerful first impression through rigorous, prior rehearsal. After all, if you're going to show up at an Open Mic Night and only get the opportunity to sing a *single* song, you want to be your *best* and outperform *everyone else* that also shows up to sing.

- *Communicate* with the crowd before and after your single song performance. Be charming, be polished and well-groomed, and behave like a "star-worthy" act. Isn't that you, anyway? It would have to be.

- Download to your smartphone the free app Creative Poster Maker to easily make a professional-looking poster for duplication. You *must* place your professional music website address on it. *Place the phrase Music Available At* just before your website address. Then have the poster in view when you perform.

- Consider getting a huge, vinyl banner designed at an office supply store that has just your professional music website address on it. Some stores will offer graphics, but you'll pay a bit more. You can bring this banner to all your shows.

- Get your poster or banner on-stage by immediately getting on the stage when the previous singer is done and walking off the stage, right before you sing. Do it quickly, or have someone do it for you. The club owner won't mind if you do this, and will see that you're *serious* about having a career.

- You want to show that you are a true talent that stands out from the rest by giving a *brief*, clever and confident greeting and immediately starting your song.

- When you perform your single song at the Open Mic Night, or develop a full live show down the road, make *full* use of the stage. If you are a singer, don't just stand in one place on the stage to sing. Move across the entire stage, using the entire space to face the audience, smile and make brief eye contact with the audience. Alternate by shifting your eye contact slightly above the eyes of the audience toward the back of the room and around it so you don't put anybody on the spot. If the stage is very small and you can't really move around that much, just naturally move your head and body language from side to side and follow the same eye contact strategies just mentioned. Regardless of the stage size, try your best to use body language in a way that makes the audience feel connected to you as a result of the feeling you are connecting with them.

- Again, smile. Make eye contact with people and smile at them if they appear to like what they see and hear.
- Have a small supply of CDs and/or MP3 download cards. At the end of your performance, before you leave the stage, tell the audience that you have these on-hand for them to purchase. Oftentimes, if you really do give the audience a *thrill* during your one song, they will immediately go home and purchase your music online since you've told them how to get their hands on it. Do this at *all* shows and not just Open Mic Nights.
- Do something different and unique from the other performers. You have all the imagination in the world to accomplish this task because you are an *artist*. You do not even need to be told "not to be like everybody else," but I am saying it anyway because competition is fierce. Make the audience think that your performance is rare and special, because it *is*.
- Emphasize the fact that the audience can join your mailing list on your professional music website when

you're done performing. Your mailing list is like virtual real estate. Email your list a brief update *once* a month. The tone in your email should be personal and make your fans feel special, appreciated and connected with you.

- You could also hold a raffle so that somebody goes home with a free CD or digital music download card. The entire reason you are performing live is to get people to *buy* your music on your professional music website or right at the show.

If you follow these suggestions and are successful at wowing the audience, club owner or booking agent, you will only have to stand *once* in the dreaded line of artists signing up on the roster sheet before an Open Mic Night begins. Why? Because, after you've wowed the audience and showed your marketing savvy for your musical product, you can simply speak with the booking agent in charge of the roster sheet after you perform and *tell* them you want to play there as an act. Most artists don't know to do this, and they are unprepared to get a "Yes." Discuss frequency with the booking agent, and *commit*. You might have just turned yourself into a "Resident Performer" at the music venue. Now you can tell the entire music industry where to find you on your professional music website and in your EPK.

Keep going. You can do it. The key thing to understand is that if you network with other performing musical talent, you can plan to headline or be included in their roster, which will expose your music to many of their fans and, perhaps, turn those fans into your own as well. You might also gain access to a club or arena that you didn't previously have access to.

# 13

## GET PUBLICITY AND RADIO PLAY USING JUST YOUR HOME COMPUTER

I am now sharing an important and highly accessible way for you to announce your new single, EP or album to the public, using your home computer. I am revealing a platform that can *continuously* announce your new music on your behalf, without any tedious work on your part, thanks to the technology at your fingertips today. After all, you are living in one of the best times in history to seamlessly start an online publicity campaign for the music you work so hard on. As the old adage goes, "Without publicity, nothing happens." You may also accomplish the task of obtaining Terrestrial FM and college radio play, as I will show you.

In my own professional experience over the years, I have found that you can create an online publicity and radio campaign that garners *surprising* results in less time than you think, using technology to "blast" your online music and promotional materials to hundreds of targeted music blogs, websites and radio stations at a time. This is the true luxury of having this technology available.

With this said, I am also *cautioning* you, also based on my own professional experience, to not bite off more than you can chew since you are just starting out. You might consider, for your own health and professional longevity in music, that getting too much press and attention before you feel ready can be too overwhelming to handle. For those of you who are eager for as much as you can get in as little time as possible, then by all means, go for it. For the rest of you talented artists, slow and steady can also win the race. Working at a calm but steady pace can often garner you more success in the long run, while enabling you to keep your wits about you. Fast or slow, I am on your side.

Below, I've highlighted some of the most effective companies and sites for getting help with publicity from your home computer.

## MusicSUBMIT.com

This is the principle company you might want to start with. They can be your primary online publicity firm to announce your new single, EP or album—plus live shows if you play live. They have been around for approximately two decades and are an indispensable asset to making your new single, EP or album known to established music bloggers who write about your specific musical style, as well as to promote you to Terrestrial FM/college radio. Oftentimes, these online blogs and music sites will even embed your music video into their own sites.

MusicSUBMIT.com has improved and fine-tuned their service so well over the years that it is astounding, all while being highly cost-effective. They created an overwhelming amount of press for my first official music release. They offer everything from a single submission to a music blog, or inexpensive, one-time online "blasts" of your music to specific, targeted music blogs and radio stations of your musical style.

What I love most is that they have also created monthly, online subscriptions for every budget imaginable so that your project gets automatically blasted every month to different, specifically targeted radio stations and blogs. You won't have to do any of this work by hand. This type of service offers you the ability to grow at a monthly pace that you can handle. There are three simple steps to getting started with MusicSUBMIT.com:

1. Go to MusicSUBMIT.com and sign up for an account.
2. MusicSUBMIT.com has its own version of the EPK you built. MusicSUBMIT calls their EPK an MPK, which stands for Music Press Kit. Take all the contents of the hard work you put into your EPK and use it in MusicSUBMIT's MPK.

Make sure you include the URL address of your professional music website within your MusicSUBMIT MPK so that both the press and the public can visit your site, *buy* your music and possibly get you *more* reviews and visibility.

1. Choose a submission package with MusicSUBMIT that fits your needs and budget. Remember, the convenience of this company is that you can choose how much press you want and how often.

SubmitHub.com

This online music submission website might work in the area of saving you *time*. I am including it not just for its convenience, but to remind you that you should also be doing some online promotion (even just one task a day) while allowing Music-SUBMIT and other online portals to work on your behalf. I already know that you are anything but lazy. With this said, you want to be doing your fair share of active work to get your music career, sales and exposure as big as you want them to be, and at a pace you can handle. This website might help you handle some of these tasks in a *much* less stressful way. There is a free and a paid version.

SubmitHub.com allows you to submit to a plethora of targeted music bloggers on your own. The difference is that all you have to submit is a single song to eager, targeted musical blogs and websites who might want to review you. You have the possibility of making an income stream through streaming of your song or songs if you use it correctly. Follow this simple, three-step procedure:

1. Instead of simply uploading a single MP3 as one of their options, you have the option to provide them with a link to your selected, single song. SubmitHub currently accepts links from SoundCloud, YouTube, Spotify, Apple Music, DEEZER, bandcamp, and audiomack—all of which you should have your music ingested into by now, or very soon.

SubmitHub allows you to submit a link from any of the above music streaming sites as an additional alternative to the MP3. If you submit a link, and a popular music blog or multiple music blogs choose your song and post your link, you stand a chance of increasing streams of your song from interested music fans who follow the blogs. If you factor in the tracking system we discussed earlier in the book that SoundScan uses to count the number of streams you've achieved and they convert into sales, you increase your chances of creating an income stream.

Whichever music streaming site link you choose, remember that music fans and music blog writers have the ability to share your link on their own fan pages and online stations. If you haven't done so already, just find your personal link to your single song by going to your chosen highlighted music streaming site and typing in your name and your song. Copy and paste the link to your chosen streaming page into Submit-Hub.com.

1. The next step is to check off all of the provided Genre Filters of music blogs that like your style of music, or *might* likely enjoy your song.

The music blogs will decide whether to review you. They receive half of the minimal fee if they choose to review you, so it is to their advantage as well as yours. Don't be afraid of the review. Regardless of the review's content, at least they chose you and embedded your music-streaming link from one of the big-time music streaming services mentioned in Step 1 within their review. If it's a good review, add it to your website, EPK and MPK! People who visit the particular music blog site might stream the song and judge for themselves whether they enjoy your song. Again, the more blogs that include your paid streaming link, the more streams you can get—and the more streams you get, the more you might be paid.

> **Take Note:** Make sure your chosen music streaming
> platform link to your song has a link to your profes-
> sional music website so that people who listen to and
> like your song on these music blogs can buy your music

if they choose to. And *please...* Make sure you do an online search to see which music streaming service is currently paying the highest, as this can always change. Just type into a search engine, "Which music streaming services currently pay the highest?"

## Ezinearticles.com

This site can really catapult the number of visitors to your professional music website through the roof—in a carefully targeted way. If you can write, or can get someone to help you write high-quality articles and news about your music and yourself as an artist, you can gain "exposure, credibility, and traffic" for your website by publishing your news on their platform. Ezinearticles.com has been around since (virtually) the beginning of the general public's access to the Internet. They are experts worth checking out. I have known of this immense writing platform for over two decades.

## Musicdish.com and Mi2n.com (Music Industry News Network)

These two are innovative, and just plain cool websites for publicity. They are cutting-edge authorities on the world of music. Mi2n.com, in particular, has a truly impressive and unique free service that blesses artists with the ability to submit their own news for free at their site, after which the company distributes it electronically to many key sources that can potentially help in the advancement of their music careers.

Mi2n.com gave me a fantastic review of my first official CD release. Through this site, you have the potential opportunity for international press—and you should know by now that press is the most important element in gaining visibility as a musical talent.

## AirplayDIRECT.com

You might also want to check out this site. They operate entirely online, have been around for quite some time, and offer many benefits for possible radio airplay. You can build an AirPlayDIRECT.com profile using the content you built within either your Sonicbids EPK or your MusicSUBMIT MPK. And on your professional music website, you can add a link to your AirPlayDIRECT profile. Your goal as an artist is to gain as much visibility as you can.

> **Take Note:** The more profiles you have with these types of press, radio and live music promotional websites you've built using direct links to your professional music website, where viewers have direct access to your Sales page, the more you will appear completely well-rounded, *established* and industry knowledgeable to the music industry-at-large, as well as potential fans looking to buy or stream your music. With these profiles, you stand a much better chance of creating more visibility as an artist and potential income streams through your precious musical talent, your new music company and your image.

## Radio-locator.com

Radio-locator.com offers a complete database of all radio stations categorized by city, state, market and format. This might prove to be invaluable for a small tour where you can contact stations in certain markets to provide them with (roughly) three weeks or more notice that you're coming into their city or town. Follow up politely if you do not hear back. You should try to arrange an on-air interview while you're playing in different cities!

## 14

---

# MUSIC LICENSING

*Licensing* your music is the process of obtaining a contract or contracts with various music licensing companies that are willing to accept your songs and use them under specific conditions in their productions. These productions can include film, television, radio commercials, video games and industrial videos aimed at both non-entertainment and entertainment-related companies.

Music licensing is, unarguably, one of the most lucrative income streams for both signed, established musical talent *and* independent or unknown musical talent. Yes, you stand a chance of getting licensed by a music licensing company, even if you are just starting out. There are literally thousands of these companies in existence.

> *Take Note:* What matters most is the quality of your music and which songs you carefully choose to present. You must also put together a professional package to give music licensing companies a great

first impression. This book is showing you how to present your songs in the most professional ways possible.

Before entering this licensing world, there are two major music licensing resource, advice and opportunity websites you should visit that offer a huge amount of education. You can easily sign up for their email lists below if you choose to:

- SyncMyMusic.com
- SilverScreenMusician.com

While at these sites, sign up on their email lists because the resources they offer and the continuous education they provide will give you further lessons on preparing your music for music licensing, providing you with information on many of the music licensing companies that exist. They do so much of the research for you because they themselves are very passionate musicians who are very successful in this arena. If you do obtain a music licensing or synchronization deal, please, always read the fine print. Do not sign anything you don't understand. You might strongly consider joining the Songwriter's Guild of America (songwritersguild.com) to inquire about aligning with a professional who specializes in reviewing music licensing contracts. The Songwriter's Guild of America (SGA) also offers song placement services in addition to many other resources. You must consider joining.

> **Take Note:** If you get signed with a music licensing company, an *exclusive* contract means your songs are locked in for the length of the contract and you will be unable to license your work to others. A *nonexclusive* contract means you can still market your songs

anywhere in the world, including to multiple, *nonex-clusive* music licensing companies.

You're the boss of your own career. Remember that. This means you get to decide which type of music licensing offer best fits *your* needs. You can always do an online search for music licensing companies. There are thousands of them. Here is a small, sample list you can research. This list is intended to show you the variety of music licensing companies in existence and the full range of musical styles that different music licensing companies cover:

freshmusic.com

fundamentalmusic.com

globalgraffiti.com

gmpmusic.com

gothic-storm.com

haveasync.com

hum.co.uk

ibaudio.com

indigimusic.com

inspiredproductionmusic.com

inthegroovemusic.com

jwmediamusic.co.uk

konsonant.com

kwiksounds.com

labhits.com

lapostmusic.com

latinpulsemedia.com

lemoncake.com

LicenseMusic.com

ligarmusiclibrary.com

liquidcinema.com

loopsound.com

luckstock.com

pro.jamendo.com/stock-music-licensing

Pumpaudio.com

uk.emiproductionmusic.com

# 15

## NETWORKING AND SONGWRITING ORGANIZATIONS

A lot of you might be going through your journey as a solo musical talent feeling like you are *alone*, doing it "by yourself." As a result, you might have a tendency to avoid or hold back on the prospect of networking with other singers, songwriters or musicians. I applaud how *tough* you are. I am very proud of you for being so strong and independent-minded as a human being, musical talent and all-around *survivor*. I can relate to the tendency people often have of being so fixed in their own independent work habits that they don't reach out to work with other singers, songwriters or musicians.

You are *not* alone. Singers, songwriters and musicians around the world experience the same kind of hesitation. But you don't have to go through your solo music journey alone. It is not healthy. It is very wise, instead, to consider networking with other artists.

I want to give you options to start networking with other singers, songwriters and musicians *in person*, and not just online. If you are too used to working alone, here is a list of carefully researched songwriting and music networking organizations where you might consider trying to place your toes gently in the water by joining or even attending a single meeting. It is *good* for you.

You can meet people at in-person meetings to network, make contacts, exchange creative ideas, collaborate or just make friends who share your same passion for music. You might even decide to become active in the actual decision-making processes of the organization(s). Or you might stumble upon a lead that, for all you know, could end up affecting the future of your music career in a very beneficial and substantial way. With all this said, at least think about taking baby steps by attending a single meeting. You can do it. I am *with* you and so is this book.

Because many of you reading this book are likely located around the world, below I've provided a list of global networking and songwriting organizations that, if you get involved, ultimately might help you grow your music career. I've included additional information for a few of these organizations that may be of particular interest.

- AFM.org (American Federation of Musicians)—This is the union for musicians that offers pension programs for live performances, musician referrals, performance venue referrals, and other production resources, including recording studios with discounted rates, and resources for shooting music videos. There are required dues to join, and there are different chapters of the AFM, according to what city and state you happen to live in.
- Aimp.org—Association of Independent Music Publishers (New York, NY)

- Alabama Songwriter's Guild, 256-352-4873
- Angelfire.com/music/ncgcsg—Gospel/Christian songwriters group
- Canadacouncil.ca—Canada Council for the Arts
- Ccma.org—Canada Country Music Association (CCMA)
- Cmrra.ca—Canadian Musical Reproduction Rights Agency, Ltd.
- Coloradomusic.org—Colorado Music Business Organization
- Composers Guild (Utah), 801-204-6331
- COSA4u.tripod.com—Central Oregon Songwriters Association
- Country Music Association of Texas, 254-938-2454
- Countrymusicassociationoftexas.com—Country Music Association of Texas
- Ctsongs.com—Connecticut Songwriters Association
- Folk.org—Folk Alliance, International
- Fwsa.com—Fort Worth Songwriters' Association (Texas)
- Gmia.org—Georgia Music Industry Association
- Gospel.org—Gospel Music Association (Nashville, TN)
- Gov.texas.gov/music—Texas Music Office
- Insound.com—Vinyl artists are featured here
- Jpfolks.com—Just Plain Folks Music Organization (Indiana)
- Junoawards.ca—Canada Academy of Recording Arts & Sciences (Canada's Music Awards)
- Lamn.com—Los Angeles Music Network (Universal City, California)
- Manitobamusic.com—Manitoba Music, Canada

- Memphis-songwriters.org—Memphis Songwriters Association (Memphis, Tennessee)
- Mnsongwriters.org—Minnesota Association of Songwriters
- Music.org—The College Music Society (Montana)
- Musicianscontact.com—Musicians Contact (regular listings of PAYING JOBS for musicians and artists looking to connect)
- Music-USA.org/nacusa—The National Association of Composers/USA (NACUSA)
- Nashvillesongwriters.com—Nashville Songwriters Association, International (NSAI)
- Pasamusic.org—Philadelphia Area Songwriters Alliance
- Portlandsongwriters.org—Portland Songwriters Association (Oregon)
- Risongwriters.com—Rhode Island Songwriters Association (RISA)
- Saw.org—Songwriters' Association of Washington
- Scmatx.org—Southwest Celtic Music Association
- Sdsongwriters.org—South Songwriters Guild (California)
- Sffmc.org—South Shore Folk Music Club
- Songwriter.co.uk—International Songwriters Association, Ltd. (England)
- Songwriters-guild.com—The Guild of International Songwriters & Composers (England)
- Songwritersguild.com—The Songwriters Guild of America (SGA) (New York, NY)—Also mentioned in the previous chapter on music licensing. This organization and site is an incredibly valuable resource for singers, songwriters and musicians.
- Songwritersinseattle.com—Songwriters in Seattle

- Songwritersofwisconsin.org—Songwriters of Wisconsin International
- Songwritersresourcenetwork.com/associations-and-organizations.php—songwriters' organizations around the country
- SongwritersResourceNetwork.com—Songwriters Resource Network (Portland, Oregon)
- Songwritersresourcenetwork—Songwriting resources and organizations across the entire U.S. continent and abroad
- Songwriteruniverse.com—Songwriting resources, organizations, publishers, record labels, clubs, publications, producers, studios galore, and personal empowerment
- Songwriteruniverse/kentuckysa.htm—songwriter associations for Kentucky, Louisiana, Maine, Maryland, and Massachusetts
- Spars.com—SPARS (The Society of Professional Audio Recording Services)
- Thefield.org (Art Grows Here)—The Field (New York, NY)
- Victorymusic.org—Victory Music
- Wamadc.com—Washington Area Music Association
- Westcoastsongwriters.org—West Coast Songwriters
- Womeninmusic.org—Women in Music

## 16

---

## GLOBAL RECORD COMPANIES

Most, but not all artists have a goal of signing with a record label for one key reason: a major record label has the resources to help you build and grow your music career to a far more substantial level. As I have noted earlier, your sales and paid streams can attract their attention. But you can also market yourself directly to them, and I will share my strategy for reaching global record labels. Keep in mind that if you choose to remain independent and run your music career on your own, this is fine too. It is *your* career and you get to decide how much growth that you alone desire or require.

***Take Note:*** Please understand that the following information is not meant for you to "cut corners" on the music marketing strategies I have taught you in this book. Instead, I think this in an additional direction that is very cool and fun to do a bit at a time, since you have so many options today when trying to find a record label to work with. Until that happens, though, remember that you still must do the work—even if it is only a single task per day—in support of growing your music career.

## Take a Global Perspective

Our instincts often tell us to think within our own countries of residence. Regardless of where you happen to live as you read this book, a huge volume of musical talent seems to focus mainly on getting a record deal in the United States. Sometimes, however, we forget something that is not only very important, but *very* exciting. We live in a *global* music market.

In 1999, American singer-songwriter and musician Tom Waits released a song called "I'm Big in Japan." He had not obtained a record deal in his own country, but was huge in Japan with his music. Thus, he wrote that song and it became a hit. With immensely clever lyrics about his own self-perceived, personal imperfections, the point he makes in the song is "you may not have heard of me here in the U.S., and my life is not perfect; however, I'm huge in another country." Now all of the U.S., and many people beyond, recognize this extremely important song from an *immensely* talented music artist and writer.

Countries like Belgium, Germany, Italy, Spain, France, England, The Netherlands and Japan have very active music industries. I only name these countries as several examples.

For an online global database of record companies, check out Allrecordlabels.com. Allrecordlabels.com is a lifesaver of a website for singers, songwriters and musicians seeking a U.S. or global record label deal. It has been around for oh-so-long. They have over 25,000 record labels across the globe within their database, and everything is organized according to music genre. Allrecordlabels.com probably has the largest and most established global record company database; however, you can always search online for the phrase "record companies around the world" or something similar, and there will be other sites that provide this type of global database if, *heaven forbid,* Allrecordlabels.com ever comes down.

## Approaching Global Record Labels

My strategy for approaching global record labels might help you catch a break with and get, at the very least, a single released through one of the labels in the global database. I cannot promise you that you will, but through my research I've developed a professional way to approach these global record labels. This is where your EPK becomes so valuable. It can be used around the globe. You have immense power, now that you're armed with an EPK. Read on.

First, you need to understand the difference between *unsolicited* and *solicited material.*

*Unsolicited material* is any music that an artist attempts to send to a label directly, without the use of a third party, such as an entertainment attorney representing the artist. Huge record companies, correctly referred to as *major labels,* always have something on their website that says, "No Unsolicited Material Accepted," or some similar phrase. They mean it. If you send unsolicited material to them, it will be returned to you.

*Solicited material* is any music that a record label will accept if submitted properly. Many smaller labels and independent labels that have the distribution power to sell your work like a major label, *will* accept unsolicited material directly from *you.* They will usually note on their website that they "Accept Unsolicited Material."

Now that you know the difference, here is the strategy I suggest for using Allrecordlabels.com to seek out a smaller or independent record deal in another country, even if you haven't sold much music yet. The rules are different according to which country you're attempting to get a record deal with, in regard to the number of sales you have made, if any at all, so carefully review the guidelines for each country you are looking to work with and in.

1. Go to allrecordlabels.com.

2. Use the **Browse** feature to find the musical style or styles that you make, because record labels generally specialize only in specific genres of music. You want a record company that specializes in *your* genre of music.

3. You also have the ability to browse for city, country and format. Format means what the record label produces, i.e.. instant downloads, records, cassettes, CDs, etc. *Take Note:* Focus on the countries and record labels that specialize in your genre(s). The list of musical styles and specialty music in the **Browse** section to browse through is *immense*. This is good.

4. For the record labels you are interested in, find out if they accept unsolicited material. If, for some reason, they don't mention it on their site, send a very polite email, asking them if they will accept unsolicited music.

5. If the website already mentions they accept unsolicited materials, send a very polite email to the label that specializes in your musical style, and ask them if you can email them your EPK (Electronic Press Kit). **Do not *ever* send your music or EPK without getting permission first.**

6. Be professional and polite in your email. Ask if you can send it, because your music genre appears to be a

good fit for theirs. You might also want to include *only* two to three sentences about yourself before asking if you can send your EPK.

7. Once you receive permission, email your EPK to that label, anywhere on the globe. How lucky you are to be able to do this!

8. When you send them your EPK, write something brief and professional to remind them who you are. If you received permission from them to send in your EPK, remind them of that. Since real people will be reviewing your EPK and music, it helps not only to be professional but also *friendly*.

9. Remember, this is a global music industry. There's a certain magic that can come from saying hello to a person at a company overseas, via email, and letting them know a little bit about you. Some independent labels might love to have heard from an artist in another country. You can build lasting relationships if you are clever and kind; even if they are not looking for your music right away.

# 17

## MUSIC MERCHANDISE

As mentioned earlier in the book, in addition to selling your music, you should create and sell a variety of music-related items. In addition to these products potentially making you some additional income, they are huge promotion opportunities —getting great visibility for your name and music.

Also, selling these products can help build your email and mailing lists. These lists can be promotional gold for you and your music, because each time you have a new song, or a live event, or anything new you want to share, you'll already have a built-in audience you know is interested in what you are announcing.

You can start creating items anytime, but as I've cautioned earlier, don't put them up for sale anywhere until you have your music copyrighted (see Chapter 3).

Here are two companies I recommend:

- **Cafepress.com**—At this website, you can set up a

*completely free* online store for your music merchandise, carrying every type of mug, t-shirt, sweatshirt and novelty item you can think of, proudly displaying your artist photo or company logo. You simply upload your images to a template of the item, create your own store and set your own prices. Plus, your Cafepress.com store's website address can be linked to your professional music website, and vice versa—you can place your professional music website's link on your Cafepress.com store's page. These are both very convenient, indeed. The company manufactures your music-related merchandise, on-demand, when a fan orders it. You can create your merchandise store using images of you, your name, your website, your artwork, a written message or anything else you want to create as a product for your name, your music or your company. Again, *remember* to put your website address on the photo, logo, or graphic you choose for your merchandise. People walking around in t-shirts or hoodies that display your website address on it are great advertising vehicles for selling your music and increasing your visibility.

- **Websticker.com**—You name it, and this website has everything you need for creating visibility of your professional music website, artist photo or company logo. You can create visibility and exposure of your music with everything from bumper stickers and decals, to labels and magnets.

Your promotional items can be given away and assist in promoting your music, or they make great gifts for fans and industry alike. You can give away stickers of your music brand or hold a promotional giveaway of them, directly from your professional music website and social media—*in exchange* for getting potential fans to join your email list, and providing their mailing address to you so they can receive the stickers or magnets.

Another great and *cost-free promotional giveaway* you can offer is a free MP3 song emailed by you to a music fan if they sign up for your email list. This is a very smart thing to do and highly recommended to initiate a connection with a new fan you can keep in touch with who might buy your music, now or in the future.

# 18

---

# PUBLICISTS, AGENTS AND MANAGERS

Congratulations! What you've accomplished so far is spectacular—because you are spectacular.

As your career and your financial resources grow, you will need different kinds of help to reach a broader audience and manage your *growing* career. At some point, you may be looking to hire a whole crew of people to support both your creative pursuits and the business of running your music career.

This chapter talks about three of the most important of these new hires—a publicist/PR (public relations) firm, an agent and a manager. Publicity/press/PR, along with a smart, connected, savvy agent and manager committed to your vision and your success can help catapult all your impressive hard work into the stratosphere for all to witness, hear—and *purchase*.

> ***Take Note:*** In a business that is surrounded with unscrupulous people who will promise you the moon and the stars in all music areas, I want to *once again*

remind you to be cautious—and do your research before choosing to work with any firm.

## Publicity and Publicists

*Publicity, public relations, press*—these are all parts of the larger umbrella of *promotion*. Something extremely important to understand is that *promotion is not something you do once. It must be an ongoing part of building your career, and your company.* At the same time, you can and *should* do it at your own pace.

## Publicity on Your Own

- In Chapter 13, I suggested you start with MusicSUBMIT.com, or something similar. You can have monthly "blasts" of your music, PR material, and presence go to music-related, online mediums that will flood the Internet and give you exposure. Each month, you'll get more exposure. The monthly fees are realistic and make the investment possible. If you have won a huge music competition or any other competition using your music, you must add it to your biography on your professional music website, to your EPK, to your MPK at MusicSUBMIT and to your social media. The press you get from them might be worth the extended, monthly subscription because your exposure *should* increase every month. As you gain positive press, you must continue to add that press to your website, EPK, MPK and social media. Keep everything current. You did the work, so you owe it to yourself (and the world to see) so they'll stream and buy your music.

- You can contribute articles and interviews to different music blogs and online news resources mentioned in Chapter 13—getting your name and your music further and further known. This is how you build a story of your act.

- Again, anytime you receive an award or specific recognition, make sure you post these accomplishments everywhere you can—by updating your professional music website, your bio, your EPK, MPK, social media and everywhere else you have it posted. Always update everything and remember what I mentioned earlier in the book how you can simply copy and paste your updates across all formats to save you time!

- You can develop your own relationships with music media, other media and reviewers through personal letters and emails. Include story slants aimed toward current and/or local events—for the local, global or cultural relevance to their readers. This is not only rather common, but routine if you follow *all* the way through with patience. Your current newspaper or online prospect doesn't even have to like your music to feature you or interview you. If they think you have something that's spreading and creating a buzz, especially sales along with shows or appearances, they will want to cover you, too. Still, be patient and always remember...they might not have rejected your news. They just might not have heard it or gotten to your submitted news update yet!

- If you are a singer, songwriter, artist or musician, find a cause that is near and dear to you.

Charitynavigator.com can help you find a legitimate charity where the money goes exactly to the people who need it most. This is part of your job as an artist. You want to make a difference, and not one based only on your music. Finally, if you get involved to raise funds for the correct charity, you may be making important connections—even when you don't realize it—while you are making a positive difference for those who need it most in our global society.

- Some people might suggest you approach a local business—maybe a car dealership or a clothing company—and offer to do shows at their place of business or advertise their logo and/or services, etc., on your marketing materials for your act in exchange for sponsorship money. Your goal of attaining sponsorship money for your act from a business is to use the money for a publicist with serious connections who can earn you prestigious shows and exposure to the movers and shakers of the business. This can be a win-win, because you get the money you need to hire the professionals you need—and your sponsor gets a worthy amount of publicity, often for not much money out of their pocket. When you approach a potential sponsor, bring your press kit and your message with you. Do not ask about emailing an EPK; they likely won't know what you're talking about. Hence, you must go in-person with the physical product. You can do this by making several, physical copies of your press kit that includes all the components of your EPK, including a CD with the songs you carefully chose for your EPK. Don't just think about car dealerships. Think about every business entity you can imagine.

- Use a website like gofundme.com and create a page asking to raise money for a publicist. Use your social media choices mentioned in Chapter 7 to help push your campaign. Tell your friends on social media and offline about your fundraiser. Tell everybody. You can even have a fundraiser at a live show if you mention it on stage and design a fancy poster for free to place on stage and back your *verbal* message, using the free Creative Poster Maker App.

## Press Releases and the Value of Press Release Writers

PRWeb is an excellent resource for putting out free and low-cost press releases. If press release writing is another of your many creative talents, that's great. If not, hiring a professional press release writer to write your releases with true newsworthy quality is genuinely worth the money.

The price for having a professional write your press release can be anywhere from $75 to $200, depending on the scope of the story. This is where I recommend you also consider alternatives. For one, you can check out fiverr.com, or you may consider a trade deal with a press release writer. The good news is that most often you will only need a short press release —maybe 500 words, or even much less. Sometimes, the shorter the press release, the greater the chances that someone from a media outlet will share the news.

The major press release distributors distribute your news to hundreds or thousands of publications, and also to Reuters and the Associated Press (AP). This is big-time. However, the national news will probably not pay attention to you unless you are announcing something that ties into the current biggest news stories of the day. So start with press releases to selected "regions" near you. This can also increase your chances of one of the larger news organizations picking up your story. Pick and choose when to send out a press release through a distribution company, because the costs can add up. Even if you could afford to do this once a month, it might drain you financially. This is why you might choose to focus on using Music-SUBMIT for now.

An ideal time to make the investment to have a professional press release writer do a news release and submit it on the international press distribution sites like the one I mentioned is when you have a career triumph. This, along with your charity that you are supporting will give you a *story*. You are not "advertising" your music. Instead, you are releasing a story that is a *genuine* news story.

I want to share a success story with you. When I achieved a sudden career triumph during international film festival circuit acceptances, finalist positions, and *wins* for a short and entirely pop/rock musical film I wrote, directed entirely, did all the graphic artwork and photography for and, most importantly, *performed* in, I had a press release writer create the release and submit it through online distribution. With one single submission, I got featured online press with so many large-scale, online publications. Shock set in when I discovered two of the *biggest* television networks in the world had picked up and run with my original news release in designated markets.

If I can do it, so can you. Just make sure you have a great musical product and a talented press release writer behind you.

At some point, you do need someone to represent you, even if it's a team doing tasks to lighten your load. It could even be a very cool independent label that completely understands the hard-working, independent talent with the solid work ethic they've just signed.

Having representation, even with a music agent, is growth. Yet, you have everything here to satisfy your beginning presence, including sales outlets and press. You have the computer to book your shows at websites like Sonicbids.com and others. Your computer can do everything in this book, including book shows for you. Your EPK gives you tremendous, GLOBAL power.

You have enough to start a full music career if you do the work. I just don't want you biting off more than you can chew. Get used to your progress before expanding. Keep your sanity and wits about you so that you *last*.


## Publicist/PR Companies

There might come a time when you want, or feel you need or are ready for a much bigger "promotional presence." In other words, it's time for you to reach audiences, promoters, and maybe major labels, and you need help getting to people or organizations you can't get to on your own. Then it may be time for a publicist or a PR firm to reach "bigger fish."

Generally speaking, a publicist has the media connections and can get things done faster. That's why they're so expensive. They often have access to television, radio shows, all written media, magazines and more. This can lead to increased sales for your music, your visibility and even a record contract. A good publicist has carefully cultivated working relationships with magazines, newspapers, television shows, even music companies and promoters. Many of these relationships are well established over a period of many years and, these various media companies begin to rely on a good publicist for good stories since they trust that the publicist will deliver the goods.

It's always great if you have a referral from someone who is working successfully with a publicist or firm—but those may be hard to come by. Try: pr.com and do an online search for other directories to get a list to research. A fairly effective person or firm can cost a lot of money—roughly, a *minimum* of $24,000 a year. You will have to research and use word-of-mouth to decide who is best to work with.

Depending on the size of the companies and the clients these firms boast about, you'll also learn right away whether the PR firm is in your budget. When considering an individual or firm to work with, make sure you develop a good rapport with them. Some publicists are very good, but if you do not "'vibe" with them, get out as fast as you can and do not give them a dime. If your gut tells you not to trust them, listen to your gut, despite what they might promise you.

Publicists are just people, so go with a person you like but who also has the media contacts you need. Ideally, choose someone nearby (unless you live in the middle of nowhere) and stay on them. Try to choose a firm that largely specializes in music and entertainment. If you get signed to a record label, you will need a PR firm to work with, as I mentioned earlier.

> ***Take Note:*** There are services that claim to offer successful record deal shopping for a fee. Avoid them. Although in rare instances some of these services might be legitimate, most will likely not be. Even if they are legitimate, you will probably spend a fortune and not earn a sales return on your investment. It is never wise to attempt a shortcut when working so hard on your

dreams. The goal of this book is to help you create sales of your music on your own. Deal shopping? Run.

Also be aware that there are music consultants out there who are fee-based and quite expensive. You may be approached by or feel like you need a music consultant, and I'm not saying to *never* hire one, but *be cautious and wary.* They might design a marketing plan for you, which *could be* helpful. Yet, they might want you to keep returning to them because they themselves have not answered all your questions. You will run to them. You will pay them. And when you mention your desire to hire a publicist, the consultant might feign the notion that you are being lazy. This is likely because the music consultant wants you to pay her/him and not the publicist. It is potentially deceptive. I was running to one myself years ago. Avoid.

## An Agent

A *music agent* is a person who is responsible for booking shows for singers and bands. Music agents, also often referred to as *booking agents* or *talent agents*, make live music happen. A good agent with well-placed connections can get a musician in front of the right audience and increase their profile. Sometimes, they can even get you an offer from a record label.

An agent who specializes in music or other talents will take a chance on your talent because she/he thinks you have something unique that can sell. You will not pay anything out of pocket if you choose to sign with one. Your agent will be paid a percentage of earnings you have earned through your music while being represented by her/him.

## A Manager

A manager, like an agent, is somebody you will never pay out of your own pocket. A good music *manager* will be organized, excellent with people and have a good understanding of the industry as it stands today. Some people pose as managers and charge hundreds of dollars for representing you or discovering you. You've just been robbed and scammed by a thief who is not a manager. A person can just as easily pose as an independent publicist or agent as well. The same fate just mentioned can also happen if you are not careful.

A manager, like an agent, will sign you if they truly believe you have something special, and that contract you sign with them will never have a fee. They are taking a chance on you and your talent. Despite the fact you have the luxury of booking gigs online, a good manager can get you into venues that you might not have access to. They can have many connections. The manager and the agent will take a percentage of any money you earn in your music career while you are being represented by them. If you have a manager or agent who is getting that percentage because you are selling, then you are doing well.

You should hope the manager or agent does make money from your work. If they have not, then you are not being successful. You aren't going to let that happen, though. That's why this book is here. Try to think of it as protection, because that's why it's been written for you. If you get a publicist, agent, or manager, it is time to work even harder and *not* a time to slack off.

> **Take Note:** It is very good indeed to be as self-sufficient in your music career as possible. However, there is no way on this earth that you can do it all yourself. If

you are the only real brains and ambition behind your solo musical act (with or without a band), then you only have the power of a solo artist, a.k.a., one human being.

When the time is right, let specialists handle the items I've taught you about in this chapter.

You are the singer, songwriter, artist and musician. You should be writing music and songs, and you should be performing, if that is your thing, as well as taking good care of yourself. Time is too valuable and short to try to do everything yourself.

# IV

## MANAGING LIFE—AND TIME —ALONG THE WAY

# 19

## TIME MANAGEMENT

No matter where you are in your music career—just starting out, are a rising star, or you are happily, nonstop busy—your time is one of your most valuable assets. Managing that time can be a challenge. You encounter certain challenges when you are so busy you barely have time to breathe. And a whole different set of challenges when you have way too much downtime.

Some of you are quite organized already, and really have it together. Your life might be going incredibly well. Even if that's the case, please know that this part of the book may still be very useful for you, too.

In the next few chapters, I'm going to share with you strategies to help you make decisions about your time, and to manage both the busy and the slow times.

Delegating—Putting Limits on DIY

I am a firm believer in the importance of being a do-it-your-selfer and taking care of anything and everything you can on your own, whenever possible. Yet, I have also learned through my own experiences that there is a legitimate danger in going overboard with this philosophy.

If you are the only *brains or ambition* in your career, and you regularly take the extra initiative to read books like this without any urging from others through your *own* self-discipline, it is often easy to become so busy wearing so many different hats, i.e., singer, songwriter, artist, writer, performer, web designer, promoter, manager, retailer, etc., it can become a vicious yet addictive cycle that you might have difficulty letting go of.

We all need to remind ourselves that we cannot, and many times, *should not* be doing everything for ourselves. Be willing to accept help from others. This is the only way that you will grow. The most important thing to keep in mind is that you are the talent. You are often the one that every other person involved in the production, or not involved in the production, wishes that they could be. Focus on writing, recording and performing music, if you perform live. It is not a crime to allow others to handle various web, social media and online promotion updates, etc., while you focus on being the artist.

Being wise enough to create a balance that enables you to politely delegate tasks to willing people does not make you a lazy person; it makes you a professional act who is very good at working with a team. When you make it big, you will have to do so anyway. Plus, who wants to always work alone?

While keeping everything mentioned above in mind, it is also important to do your research when asking for and hiring help.

Sadly, there are people out there who just want to take your money, and not do the work, and people who try to pass themselves off as experts in the music industry...when they are definitely *not*. This can be especially true of promoters, labels, agents, managers, or so-called consultants—all of which I discussed in the previous chapter.

Unfortunately, there are, arguably, more scammers in this business than there are legitimate people. You must learn the difference and know the difference, as this can be a very dirty business, indeed; unless you navigate it slowly and by your own schedule.

One of the hardest decisions most people have about delegating is—when to spend the money and when to DIY. Please know that sometimes, it is okay to spend money on things that will save you precious time if you choose—or things that you just don't have the expertise to do well.

The other challenge some people have with delegating is when you feel no one can do it—whatever *it* is—as well as you can. You may be right, but sometimes the trade-off of having help for freeing you up to concentrate on your music is well worth it.

> **Take Note:** You might have heard the business term Return on Investment (ROI). This a fancy term for a basic, formulaic question—will what you pay ultimately be worth your investment? And *investment* can refer to money *or* time. Each time you are trying to decide between DIY or paying for help, you can ask yourself if paying someone else—to save you time—is worth the investment.

For example, if you see yourself as (generally) clueless or fashionably challenged, you really should get an enhancement on your appearance for the stage and, perhaps, in general.

Web updates, and other costly ventures, including in terms of your valuable time, will also be saved if you pay for services with discretion and have fully examined and thought the decision through, prior to the commitment. I have previously discussed in areas throughout this book that a talented student, friend (or other gifted individual in this area) might help you with this for free or in exchange for inclusion in their professional portfolios. Please, try not to forget what I suggested earlier in the book about creating a *trade-deal*. They can be very beneficial for both people.

One thing to consider about being a loyal do-it-yourselfer is that if you get too locked into it, the old habits will die hard. A truly successful act has an agent, manager, lawyer, publicist, stylist, web designer, manufacturer, distributor and on and on and on. The divine beauty and spirit that is embedded within your genuine talent can be found in your ability to inevitably do all these things yourself *in the beginning*. Just remember that the most important thing left out here, yet which suffers the most from neglect, as you switch from hat to hat to hat, is your *music,* and making sales.

This is why it is important to find talented people, and creative ways of inspiring others to help as you implement ways of delegating jobs to them. And there are additional benefits—personally, professionally—as you build solid working relationships with friends and new kindred spirits, which can be incredibly rewarding.

## "Automate" Your Physical World

Whether you are at a point of delegating or not yet, as I said, your time is very valuable—and it's important to use it to your best advantage. One way to simplify your life and save time is with *automation*. As a creative artist, that might sound contrary to your personality and style, but please take my word that a little automation actually gives you more energy to focus on that all-important creative side.

If you follow my suggestions, I think you will realize how "freeing" it is when you concentrate, master and "automate" the things that you can control in certain areas of your creative life, rather than give so much as a breath of acknowledgement to the things we cannot control, or have trouble controlling at times. This bonus chapter focuses on things in your life that you *can* control, and not the things that you *cannot* control.

Think about this: We do not have to remember to breathe. We just do it. We do not have to remember to pump blood from our hearts to every area of our bodies. We just do. Every metabolic and physiological function necessary to your earthly survival is "automated" and working at proper throttle.

This is the idea I have in mind when it comes time for automating the immediate physical world that you personally occupy, wherever that happens to be, and getting the environment to work for you, so that you are free to work on your musical masterpieces.

When certain things are automated in your life, a once unattainable level of peace and balance can be achieved, along with concrete results if you are consistent. Creativity usually follows, which is the antidote to writer's block of any kind. In short, the goal of automation is to get your environment to work for you, and not the other way around.

One simple example of automation is direct deposit. If you are fortunate enough to be paid by your employer or clients this way, you know what a time saver it is. With direct deposit, you don't have to take time away from your creative work to travel to the bank to make your deposit. Direct deposit is automated, usually lightning-fast, and on-time. It works for *you*, and you do not work for *it*.

Automated deductions from phone and utility companies also work for you, saving you the price of a stamp and a trip to the mailbox. Your life is a bit easier, and slightly more convenient because of these services.

These are small examples of automation. In previous chapters, I've talked about other forms of automation—such as streaming services, options for posting to several media sites at once, and more—all aimed at improving the quality and sense of control you have toward the accomplishment of your musical goals.

If you have ever experienced true inconsistency in your music career or even just your day job, as well as within your emotions and feelings, then you understand that the general organization of your physical world often appears to faithfully *collapse* around you when your physical world is not organized.

These unfortunate periods of discouragement that so many singers, songwriters, musicians and artists encounter are often the principle reasons why automation of one's *physical* life can serve so infinitely well, especially in this business. You are both the personal manager and the business manager of your own life and your music career. The *two* should and can be *one* if you are organized.

Automated tasks in your physical world will carry you through your periods of discouragement and inconsistency. The result will be that inconsistency becomes more and more of a thing of the past for you. You will feel a sense of control and security you have not experienced before towards your creative work.

I know you can do this. And you will see your productivity—and creativity—return and rise, faster than you might think.

## Handling Downtime

We have all been through it. I'm talking about those times in our lives when we are either a bit rundown from stress or in-between jobs and nothing seems to be happening *fast* enough in our music careers. You may be very discouraged and have become distracted from achieving at least one goal each day to promote your music. Apathy might kick in, although I hope this is not your case. If it is, try to take some solace in the fact you are anything but alone. There are piles of people around you in the same boat. Let's get you out of the boat and into a yacht, or at least a very upscale life preserver for the time-being.

You are too *talented* and *bright* not to care. Not everybody is qualified artistically to pick up a book like this.

When we're feeling discouraged and not motivated, in addition to not advancing our music careers, we also neglect to keep an orderly living environment at home.

If you happen to be brewing with creativity, which is likely the case if you're reading this, yet you keep a very messy, disorganized environment, the chances are likely you are a creative genius. A fertile imagination can do this. Research shows that a messy and disorganized personal environment, managed by a highly creative mind, is often the mark of a genius. Take some pride in this.

At the same time, research also shows that the more organized your environment is, the more productive you can be.

You've probably heard experts say that being surrounded by clutter zaps your energy. Well, those experts know what they're talking about. You don't need to live in a spotless home, with nothing out of place, but the more clean, organized and uncluttered your environment is, the more productive you are.

I know, easier said than done. When we're down because things aren't going well, it's hard to care about cleaning or anything so "mundane" as that—plus, that isn't advancing your career. The solution...do *something* positive and productive! And you can start by preparing for when your career *does* start picking up steam.

So let's get your house in order—literally.

Get Ready

Let's start with what I refer to as "The Seven Day Rule of Appearance." In a book about building a music career, you might wonder how this section fits into that plan, but stay with me. Everything I'm telling you is indeed to help you prepare for and build your success.

If you are at home, I want you to stop what you are doing and immediately go arrange/lay out seven days of clothing for the week ahead. If you don't have seven days worth of clean clothing, then you are just minutes away from doing a load of laundry. It does not matter what day of the week it happens to be as you read this; *just do it.*

If you are not home right now, then as soon as you get home—or minutes after—go to your room and lay out seven days' worth of clothing—shirts, pants, jeans, shorts, skirts, dresses, underwear, socks, belts, shoes, watch, jewelry, glasses and anything else that completes your dressing for the day.

Once you have chosen seven days' worth of clothing, you will make sure that the clothing is hidden from the general environment of your daily life *within* your home. Put them in your closet, neatly folded or hung on hangers, side by side, or on any shelf or space in your home that you have available. You can even use a cardboard box if that's what you have to work with. Just stash the box so that it is hidden from your main living space. In other words, just as one probably does not like to leave the vacuum cleaner in the open and in plain sight after using it, you will also find a clever place to organize and store your seven days' worth of wardrobe.

Feel free to plan up to a month's worth of clothes or more in advance. I realize that might be a bit unrealistic, but do it if you can or are *willing* to. Taking about an hour or so to plan this will save you from one more annoying ritual as you race around at the last minute trying to find clothing to get together on one particular day. And as a bonus, you will have cleaned up the clutter of piles of clothes.

If you are on a low budget, or no budget, and do not have a full seven days' worth of clothing, do not despair. You will rewash the items that you need to rewash. Hand washing a few shirts or pairs of socks and ringing them out to air dry a few days in advance will cost you nothing. You will know beforehand what you need to put on in the morning, even if you think you do not have a job, or a place to go.

Now, I realize that, as an artist, you dress the way you feel inspired to dress. This is precisely the way it should be, at least for the stage. However, if you look at your career as a business, which I hope you do, even if you write and record songs to sell without performing, you still will be meeting with professionals who are necessary to your success in music. If you get your clothing organized on a weekly basis, you might be more likely to *push* for those meetings since you will feel more confident with your appearance. You will dress like a professional, even if it's smart casual.

### Straighten Up

Now that you have your wardrobe in order, let's move to cleaning up clutter in the rest of your home—and studio, if you have one.

In an ideal world, you would now go pick up and organize every bit of clutter in your home. But that's not always realistic. Unfortunately, your *available time* doesn't always coincide with your *motivation*.

One of the keys—in cleaning and most other things in life—is to not get overwhelmed. That's when most people fall into nonaction. Break down your tasks into smaller chunks. Success builds more success, and as you complete each task with a sense of satisfaction, you will be motivated to do more.

Below are a few ideas on how to arrange cleaning time that works for you. Some people work better by task, and some by time, so pick the ones that you know will work for you—or try them all. You might be surprised by which ones work best for you.

- **Clean by task**—Pick one drawer, closet or pile of papers, for example, at a time, and just work on cleaning that. Clean it, put away and organize what you need to, and give away or throw away what you don't need.

- **Clean by time**—Decide on a cleaning time—time of day and length of time. For example, set a timer and clean for 15 minutes—every day, or several days of the week. When the timer goes off, you can keep cleaning or stop, but you will enjoy a satisfaction of completing what you set out to do.

Don't stop at just your living environment. Tackle your musical instruments or recording equipment, that huge pile of cords, adaptors and gadgets that fell out of your closet when you opened it. This has happened to me more than once. If your studio environment is messy, decide to always keep it organized and free of loose equipment and items that don't belong in a studio—and make that a reality.

A cluttered environment clutters a person's *focus* on their work! You will find that hugely successful executives and highly productive people *get the edge* over the competition by being organized, both at home and in their careers. If you think and behave like a highly successful executive and musical talent, you will be ahead of many other musically talented individuals trying to make it in the music industry.

Clutter distracts and creates avoidance of tasks in many people. Take pride in what you have by keeping it organized. You'll be pleasantly surprised at how being organized motivates you—and how much better you *feel* about yourself each day.

## 20

---

# JOB ASSISTANCE IF YOU ARE OUT OF WORK

Even when your career isn't growing as fast as you'd like, it's important for you to believe—to *know*—that you can still have an amazingly fulfilling life, a successful music career and happiness in all of your creative goals. You can even have it more so than many others, despite what you might be going through. You deserve it. You are an artist. You are a *star*; get it!

And part of "getting it," means sometimes having to arrange your life to fit your music career goals. Sometimes that means working at non-musical jobs—and that's just fine, because you are doing what you need to do to live the life you deserve.

In today's financial climate, unfortunately, many people need to have more than one job to survive. This is particularly true for artists. And the types of jobs that work well for artists can be different than for other people. It may be important for you to have nights free to play live, or to have afternoons free to work with a studio, sound engineer or other musicians. The importance for time flexibility means you may need to look for part-time jobs instead of full-time, or freelance work instead of work you are scheduled to be present for on specific days and specific times.

If you have a job now, you *could* skip to the next chapter. However, you might want to consider reading this chapter anyway in case you find yourself out of work or decide you want to pursue a different kind of job.

In this chapter, I'll help you prepare a résumé and offer suggestions on where and how to apply and land the job you want.

> ***Take Note:*** There is no shame in earning an honest dollar while you take the time to get your life and musical priorities in order, even if you have to settle for something that is below your educational level or skills. Whatever you decide to do, don't *ever* give up on your dreams. Put one foot in front of the other and just stay on course.

## Résumés

It is amazing how many people do not have jobs and do not have a resume. Creating a résumé is another one of those tasks that can feel overwhelming. Fortunately, you have options for help. Read on.

### Résumé Templates

I had a computer professor at college who used to tell students to avoid preloaded résumé templates provided by word processing programs. She complained that preloaded résumé templates that allowed you to fill in your work experience exactly in the areas of the template pointed out for you were somehow *bad*. I disagree.

There is no need to reinvent the wheel. If you choose a résumé template in Microsoft Word, your months or years of procrastinating over how to create a résumé can be over in less than an hour.

Résumé templates offer you choices on styles and formats with sample areas of work experience prefilled as examples to show you how your résumé will look once it is complete. Once you choose the style and template you want, you simply delete the sample text, and replace it with your own educational, work and life experiences.

People do not have the time to analyze how you create your résumé. Think back to when we were figuring out ways to bring old songs back from the dead and using unconventional though necessary recording tactics in order to accomplish this. Just like your songs, no one will know or care how you created your résumé if you take the time to do it *well*. You can find many résumé templates free online.

## Résumé Writing Services

I used professional résumé services right out of college, just as you can now if you can afford and are willing to pay for them. There are a lot of these services available, and they can be appropriate to use if you are searching for high-level jobs, but these services are usually expensive. If this is the way you want to go, you can search online for "résumé services."

Thankfully though, we are in the age of companies like Fiverr.com. Fiverr has grown into a full-service freelance marketing suite where extremely talented artists and creative professionals, *including* résumé writers, can do amazing work for you, *starting at five dollars*. You might even consider becoming a freelancer yourself on Fiverr, offering vocal, songwriting and music services to Fiverr's global marketplace. I will expand on how you can use your musical talent to earn money on Fiverr in this section of the book.

## Ideas on Where and How to Make Money

In this online age, knowledge is of particular power when it comes time for landing a job. And more and more jobs are landed online than ever before. But online is not the only place to find work.

### Local Online Searches

There are a number of national and international online job sites—some of which I describe in the next section—that can be very helpful in your job search. But the best place to start is with the online version of any major newspaper in the city where you live. If you are in a city like Los Angeles, the *L.A. Times* Job Search area of their website is free, meticulously categorized, and most importantly, localized (as opposed to those hugely competitive national job search websites). If you are in New York, use the *New York Times* Online, and if you are in any other city in the country, use the online version of your local city newspaper's Help Wanted section. You can also Google your city along with the phrase "job fair" if you'd like to attend one.

### Online Job Sites

There are a ton of sites where you can start an online job search right away—and more are popping up all the time. While many of these online job sites offer a variety of jobs, some are particularly valuable for musical artists. What kinds of music-related jobs/gigs can you find online? Here are some ideas:

- **Fiverr.com,** once again, is the global marketplace for creative talent of all kinds, with oh-so-many opportunities for musicians, songwriters, singers, performers, and anybody who has musical talent and uses it as a passion within their lives. You can set up an account through them and become a freelancer, making side income from your home. With time and dedication in setting up your Fiverr profile and finding the keywords for services within Fiverr that customers are looking for, you could create a steady, side income with Fiverr. In closing, each and every possibility mentioned that a customer might need are things that you might need if you become a customer yourself, hiring a freelance musician, singer, or artist to assist you with working on and completing an unfinished masterpiece of your own that requires other talent. You can work with people around the globe! Most importantly, you should be using your own musical talent to become a freelancer so that you can create a steady, side income doing what you love.
- If you're a singer, you can do vocals for instrumentalists who send you their songs with lyrics through the Fiverr console if you sign up for Fiverr.
- You can also do video singing telegrams as gifts for customers who send such serenades as gifts to their sweethearts and loved ones through Fiverr.
- As a musician, you can take a customer's song, sent to you as an acapella vocal, and create the actual music for them if they don't play instruments. Think Fiverr.
- In Fiverr, you can even offer specific services such as the ability for customers to send you their unfinished instrumental track online through the Fiverr console, where you can add drums, piano, guitar, or any type

of instrumental or engineering services, including mastering services, that you have talent with or specialize in.

- As a songwriter, you can even write lyrics for customers who send you instrumentals but do not write lyrics. You can even perform them on the instrumental in your home studio and send the completed project back to your customer. There are many instances where you can charge additional fees for licensing the finished product to them within Fiverr.

The possibilities are endless for any type of musical artist. Here are some more excellent sites for you to start with:

- **Careerbuilder.com** boasts an electronic search agent, available free of charge, that can automatically email you job prospects on a weekly basis, based on your search criteria. If you do not have a résumé to upload, you can build one directly on their site.
- **Gigmasters.com** is a company that hires musicians, singers and artists of all types. You can perform at weddings, as a cover band, or as an original artist by a hired party or event where you can get paid for being hired talent and doing what most of you love doing most: performing! This is spectacular because you can do this type of work for income and as a job while you continue to create and promote your own original songs/albums. Musicians and artists have sought out gigmasters long before the days of the Internet.
- **Indeed.com** is a website that is very popular for finding part-time or full-time work at a variety of skill

levels. You can create a résumé online with Indeed.com if you do not have one, or you can upload a résumé if you do have one. You have the option to keep your résumé private or make it public so you can receive emails as jobs become available. Even if you decide to keep your résumé private, you can still get targeted job leads emailed to you on a regular basis, based on your selected job specialties/skills.

- **Livetrigger.com** currently states on their site, "Book more shows. Find more venues. Find more bands." These statements all refer to you! Look into Livetrigger and see if you can utilize it to get booked and perform more shows at more locations, network with other bands for the purpose of creating music together or performing with them as an opening act or the main act, and see what production services might be available for you to offer as a means of gaining income and increased visibility. As mentioned throughout many areas of this book, be sure to place those shows on your website, EPK, MPK and social media to enable fans to buy tickets online through your website or at the live event. You may also find other musical talent to network with, become friends and allies of in the community, where they might be able to help you polish up your own recordings.

- **Monster.com** is a website where you can apply for jobs worldwide. It has evolved as one of the largest online "job boards" in existence today. As they say on their website, they are "a global provider of a full array of job seeking, career management, recruitment and talent management products and services." Monster.com does require you to upload a résumé.

They will even review your résumé and give you feedback if you choose.

- **Snagajob.com** is a website where you can conveniently apply online for part-time or full-time, hourly paid jobs at many of the major retail businesses and shops you have often heard of. If you decide to register with Snagajob.com, you only have to fill out an application once, and it is good for all job areas you apply to. This is the kind of online job portal that is great if you are new in town or need to earn cash quickly.

- **Upwork.com** is another very well-known site where you can freelance your musical talent and build a side income. You will be able to market your talent and utilize the talents of others, just as you can with Fiverr. You should consider developing an Upwork account along with a Fiverr account to increase your chances of making more income by freelancing your musical skills.

- **Freelancer.com** is an oasis for freelancers. When asked on their website what kind of work you can get when you sign up with them, their answer is "anything you want." They are proud to have experts from every professional, technical, and creative field.

You can accomplish everything I have just mentioned without leaving your home, thanks to your home computer.

*Take Note:* Beware of any jobs that look like scams or that ask you to meet someone in a private, unconventional place. Be safe.

## People Want to Help

I am a firm believer in the basic goodness of all people. If you are in a slump, I believe it is perfectly okay to let people know, as long as you use discretion. If you are looking for a new job or freelance/contract work, networking with friends, family or anyone else you meet can be the best way to start a whole new positive chapter for you and your finances. (In the next chapter, I will be showing you ways to handle your finances for your whole life).

There are so many social networking sites available that it is truly mind-boggling. For now, just let everybody know you are looking for work, and that you have a résumé.

I have landed jobs in the past by telling people the truth about my own life and circumstances. You should too. For example, your neighbor, who works at a company that is looking for employees, might appreciate your warm and honest account of your situation. I had to use this strategy to land a job long ago, and you can too. My neighbor even recommended me for the job.

Obviously, do not tell people anything negative about your life when you are *applying* for a job through one of the national or online local city newspapers, and when making your friendly follow-up phone calls. You have a whole world outside your door to meet people and tell them your story—people who are *not* potential employers.

## Teach Music or Vocal Lessons

While this may seem obvious, I'm here to remind you that you have the opportunity to teach a musical instrument or vocal lessons if you are comfortable and experienced enough to teach what you love. Today, you can teach people in-person *or* online.

## Work as a Temp or Substitute

I also recommend the idea of being an Office Temp. It's not for everyone, but it can be just the ticket. You'll be in a professional environment as an on-call team member and you will likely make more than the standard minimum wage because of the caliber of companies you might be sent to. The temp agency knows you are into other interests, and you aren't considered either part-time or full-time staff; you're just on-call. Do a great job so they'll send you out for more work. And do your best to save some of that money. When you are in a financial position to stop temping, ask the company to take you off their list. If you need to temp again and not too much time has passed, you can tell them you're available again and they will likely put you right back on the list.

Substitute teaching is also a great option for singers, song-writers and musicians because the days and hours can be flexible, and the pay level is (generally) higher than minimum wage. Plus, you can get retirement points, even if you're just working part-time. (I'll cover more about pensions and retirement plans in the next chapter).

## The Best Ways to Follow Up

While getting a job through one of the mega-sized websites out there might seem like a lottery, your chances of success increase dramatically if you are wise enough to simply pick up the phone and do a polite and friendly follow-up about the status of your résumé. When you have applied for a job on Monster.-

com, for example, you can follow up to the *specific* company you applied to through Monster.com, on a weekly basis. Making that wise phone call is so important. Do not wait for them to call you, because you most likely will not hear from them, due to the number of résumés competing for their attention.

By simply making the decision to pick up the phone and speak with someone about the specific position you have applied for, letting them know you have sent a résumé and that you are wondering if anyone has had a chance to review it, you will be doing something that sets you apart from thousands of other job applicants. Just make sure you mention what the position is, and any job number associated with the position.

Most people haven't followed up with a friendly phone call—or not followed up at all on the résumé they submitted—and if they did do a follow-up of any kind, they did it through email.

> ***Take Note:*** Email, in my opinion, is less than satisfactory as a form of follow-up, particularly with a large company, and should only be used as a supplement that will thank the person who assisted you over the phone. If you do send email, make sure your email is friendly, cooperative, intelligent and easy-going.

Most, if not all, of the companies that list jobs on these large websites, will not ask you to call them. Some might not even leave a phone number. Unless the job listing blares the words "No phone calls," I highly encourage you to look up the phone number of the company yourself and give them a friendly phone call.

> ***Take Note:*** Developing rapport with the person who

answers the phone, or the administrative assistant for the department you're calling is often the best situation that you can create. There's an old saying that if the receptionist doesn't like you, you won't be working there. Be persistent but polite.

It might take a few weeks or more, but that polite follow-up on the phone might inspire the receptionist or admin assistant to get the ball rolling. The person might recommend that the hiring department call you in based on your professionalism and the pleasure they've had speaking with you and getting to know a little bit about you.

## Extra Cash

For some quick extra cash, you might be able to sell unused and unwanted, "previously loved," possessions. Here are two free mobile apps that can help—and there are more popping up all the time:

- letgo
- OfferUp

These two smartphone apps enable you to take pictures of your items for sale, write a description, set your price, and target others in your city who use these apps. People will answer if they are interested. You can also buy used items you might need on either of these apps. Remember that, above all, when meeting a customer, hold the meeting in a *public* place that you mutually agree upon, such as the front of a large retail store, during the day.

## A Final Note on Employment

One final and crucial piece of advice regarding employment: Oftentimes, it is in your best interest to get a retail or restaurant job, full-time or part-time, or any other job where the company understands that you are doing other things.

If you are dealing with big corporations and have a résumé for seeking a *career*, you might have to specify part-time instead of full-time, as most companies see you as an investment, and want you to be with them for the long haul. They do not want to hear about any other creative career pursuits, which, for you, would be that of a highly successful singer, songwriter or musician.

Taking a corporate part-time job, which might not be easy to get, will free up your own time and also give the correct, upfront, and above all, *honest* impression that you are pursuing other things. You do not want to get a job with a big company under the wrong impression. It is not the correct thing to do, and you do not know if there will be tension or a future problem if you were to work with a large corporation in the future.

This is a serious issue regarding your integrity, so avoid it. As a true artist, you probably have more integrity than most to begin with. Overall, the smartest thing to do to save you time when looking for work at an online job website is to type "part-time," or "contract work" into the search phrase box so that only those types of jobs reveal themselves.

> ***Take Note:*** It can be better to take the kind of job that has a high turnaround rate to begin with, so that when you quit the job and begin to see your name in lights,

there will be no problems with the employer. It is highly important to leave a *good impression* with your employer at all times, even if you eventually quit your job and move on. If you behave like a "class act" with your employer from start to finish, you can leave on good terms and may be able to work for that employer again if you need to in the future. Also, leaving a good impression can strengthen your professional reputation. Leaving a bad impression will do the opposite.

# 21

---

## FINANCIAL EMPOWERMENT FOR LIFETIME SUCCESS

Here is a subject you might feel you don't need to pay much attention to right now, given your choice to pursue an entertainment career path that harbors a lot of ups and downs.

You might hold onto the idea that many people in your life are, or have been, putting you into the category of a "struggling artist." The reality is that, if you use this term within your own life at all, the chances are substantial that you alone are using it, and no one else is even making such a distinction.

You might even believe it is expected of you to be living hand-to-mouth and, thus, creating a self-fulfilling prophecy. You run the danger of actually maintaining this belief system and lifestyle because you think you do not have a choice. Yet, you *do* have a choice, and you know it. *It's mind over matter.* You need to believe you *are already successful.* I don't want you in financial danger, so *please* learn from my experience.

I want you to *remind yourself* that you are running a business, and this means that you should be thinking like a professional.

In part, this means you really ought to be paying attention to money and retirement savings, including in areas beyond your songwriting and/or performance career. The goal here is to achieve "the big time" financially, even when you are experiencing the downtime in your career.

Just as I want you to succeed in your music career, I'm going to also help you reach financial success. First and foremost, I want you to know, believe and do this:

No matter your age, it is important to start saving.

It is important to start saving as early as you can—for living and for retirement. If you are at an age where you might think that it is too late to start, you can and must anyway. Please allow me to share with you some strategies that will convince you that it is *not* too late. Your financial security, regardless of your age, is paramount to your survival and overall health.

> ***Take Note:*** Other than any professional financial advisors you work with, tell no one, or only a few trusted people about your financial plan. Disregard the notion that people think or speculate about your lifestyle or career. You deserve to hear—often—that you have an amazing gift! You don't want your life to go by and have major regrets that you didn't pursue your musical dream and get your talent out there simply because people who were either worried about you, or just jealous, made you move in a different direction by scaring you with the threat of poverty. Get that out of your head if it is in there.

In this chapter, I'm going to show you ways that you can still have all the things you want, and let the world know you are a consummate entrepreneur in addition to a highly creative performer and all-around genius. These ideas might sound simple, and I am praying that they not only do, but that you will implement these simple ideas.

## Pay Yourself First

That's right. It all starts with paying yourself *first*. You pay yourself first for two specific purposes—you have to survive to work and grow and you need to *save* for the future. Pay yourself any amount you can afford each month, then use the rest of your money each month to pay your bills.

I can hear some of you saying something like, "I can barely afford food and rent, I can't afford to save anything." I hear you, but *please* trust my guidance. Even if you can only save a few dollars a week or month, do it. In addition to having money as a backup, you are developing a great habit for building financial health.

Money cannot buy you happiness, but it can buy you freedom, some inner peace, and most importantly, choices. Freedom and inner peace are virtually without any borders. If you do not believe me, ask a world traveler who can afford such a lifestyle.

Handle your emotions and personal relationships separately from your finances if you ever hope to amass any money.

## Savings Accounts

Opening a savings account is great for your self-esteem and your survival. It has the potential, in less time than one thinks, to blossom into peace of mind for you. The truth is that you should already have a savings account by now, ideally, for a minimum of 6–12 months of emergency living expenses. If you already have a savings account...*good*.

But why stop there? If you already have a savings account (again, you should), here is some insight on the best way to grow a savings account, and what it should be used for as you save throughout your life. Use the same patience with your savings as you do when waiting for media folks or promoters to speak with you about your music. Make the art of saving effortless or as close to effortless as possible, so that you do not even miss the money.

Saving is like planting a tiny little seed in order to grow a very strong and healthy tree. This does not happen overnight though. Be *thankful* for this. If you nurture an initial savings seed gently, it will grow without effort, automatically, and mostly without your attention. You may find that you have grown up a bit, too.

> **Take Note:** Especially when you are young, and even more so if you are struggling financially, it can be hard to think about your finances for 30, 40 or 50 years from now. But *now* is the time to begin. Life is unpredictable, and being prepared gives you, and possibly your family, and your career, a powerful strength.

A simple savings account with a competitive interest rate will do just fine. This is something you can set up that does not require much research or effort. In a world where banks rigorously compete for your business, go with the bank that offers the most competitive interest rate.

And if you're comfortable with online banking, don't forget to check them out. They often have savings accounts available that pay a higher interest rate than brick-and-mortar banks. You can look up the latest interest rates offered by financial institutions and compare them at websites such as bankrate.com. The goal is never to think about tapping into your savings, at least not for quite a period of time.

Here is a simple strategy that might help: Start with saving $100 per month, which is something you should be able to stick with. If you have to do less, then do less, but make sure you do it. Saving $50 a month is okay—$100 is just *better*. Free of charge, you can visit bankrate.com to compare interest rates for savings accounts, credit cards and many other financial categories.

As strange as it sounds, you might actually want to avoid putting any extra money each month that you might have available at the time into your savings account. Use "extra" money to pay off your debts. Just add the same amount of water, fertilizer and T.L.C. to your savings tree each month. Again, if you put too much money in, you might end up having to withdraw from the account due to unexpected expenses, debt and *temptation*. The tree could die, and you might have to start all over again with a tiny new seed. What a horrible thought, indeed.

If you are scratching your head at this point because you earn enough income each month to put away *more* than $100 or $50 each month, or you are struggling financially but believe you will be able to make the choice of cutting out unnecessary types of spending, then, by all means, put away more money each month! The most important part of the strategy is to *decide and commit to a specific dollar amount each month*, and you must commit *indefinitely*. If, during one month, you need to put in less of a deposit, do not be hard on yourself, because you are still taking care of the tree. But then get back on track with your savings plan.

Think about what kind of savings you will have in just five years if you contribute just $100 each month into an account with compounding interest. I will soon be showing you ways to potentially turn this money into much more, and perhaps, in much less time than only a monthly savings plan.

If you are living hand-to-mouth and do not know how to get out of debt, make sure the goal of your savings account is *not* to pay off your debt. Handle paying off the debt separately. Your savings account is *yours to keep*. The savings account is not used to pay bills because you are paying *significantly* less into the savings account each month and using a much larger amount of money to pay off your bills.

> **Take Note:** If you have credit card debt on more than one credit card, pay off the higher interest rate cards first. For example, pay just a little over the minimum required amount on lower interest cards while you pay more on the highest interest card.

Many savings accounts offer automatic, monthly withdrawals from a checking account (or other account) directly into your savings account. Although I talked earlier about automating, when it comes to your savings account, I recommend, instead, going each month and making your savings deposit to the bank in-person, if that feels right to you. The trip to the bank will give you time to visualize your dreams as you experience genuine self-confidence in that moment when you go to the bank to make your deposit. You are a responsible adult who actively participates in the construction of a solid financial future, and one who makes these wise decisions because you care about yourself, your loved ones and your future goals. This is an errand worth a bit more of your actual time to feel good about yourself.

## Goals for Your Savings

I also suggest having a savings goal beyond that of a safety net. Think of it as resources to attain other goals in your life. There are a variety of other options for potentially building your financial strength—some safer or riskier than others.

### *Property—Really*

If you are currently renting an apartment, once you've built up your savings, you might want to think about using a good portion of your savings account for a future down payment on a home or a production/recording studio. Better yet, you might think about a down payment on a future home in which you will *also* build a recording studio. I like this idea better.

Buying a home and/or investing in a studio can be a wise investment. Property and land, *in general*, tend to go up in value, and not down, as the years pass. Some artists put a down payment on a recording studio that has creative space for sleeping, eating and living, without having to reveal anything to your clients or others who see you as a recording studio, record label or production company. Right after college, I interned for a recording studio and independent record label in New York City, like the one I just described.

### *Stock Market Investment Accounts*

Investing in the stock market can be risky and I advise working with a financial advisor. Be sure you understand how the advisor is paid as that can cut into your earnings. If you have experience in investing and the time and skills to research and understand the fluctuations of the market...so you absolutely feel you can invest on your own, you already know you should still *research, research, research* before you invest.

Investing in the stock market does not necessarily mean buying individual stocks. There are a variety of instruments that range in risk, such as mutual funds and index funds. I'm not recommending any specific strategies or experts. However, these are a few respected resources that many people refer to for guidance and education:

- *Money Magazine.*
- Online versions of newspapers like *The Wall Street Journal* will offer you investing tips. Today, many of these publications are free if you read the online version, or they cost about a dollar or so a month.
- Experts such as Warren Buffet and those whose experience and reputation are similar to his.
- Companies such as Kiplinger and Morningstar that rate stocks, funds, and other investment instruments, and make their findings available for free on their websites.

If you *do* decide to invest on your own, you might want to get started by visiting a site such as Directinvesting.com. There, you can begin investing from the comfort of your own home, using your computer. Do not go it alone when doing any of this. Follow the guidance of experts. They are right there on the site for you.

### *Retirement Accounts*

An extremely important savings and planning strategy is the establishment of a *true retirement account—or more than one.* You should start a retirement account in addition to your savings account. Together, these will carry you nicely over time. You may want to find an Adult Education program in your area for a course covering retirement savings. Adult Education is not expensive, and the teachers are often pretty magnificent. Below are a few ways of providing for your retirement that you might consider.

## Pensions

Some companies—though not as many as there used to be—provide you with a pension when you retire. So do some temp and substitute teaching jobs. But you should not rely solely on a pension for a number of reasons. For one, you may have to work at a company for a very long time to be eligible for a pension—and we hope that instead, your time will be spent on your successful music career. As a part-time employee, temp worker or substitute teacher, it could take you *sixty or more years* to have a pension large enough to retire on comfortably.

## 401ks

In addition to, and instead of a pension, many companies offer what is called a 401k retirement plan. And some of these are set up so that your employer will match what you contribute. For example, if you contribute $25 a month from your paycheck to the company 401k, the company contributes a matching amount—an additional $25 per month up to a pre-set limit. But do not assume that your 401k or retirement plan is enough. You should learn more about what a 401k is and what it is not.

## Simple IRAs and Roth IRAs

Many experts feel that the *ideal* situation is to save for retirement through an Individual Retirement Account, or IRA. That is because IRAs are independent of your job status.

***Take Note:*** Find out if your 401k plan at work can be "rolled over" into your Roth IRA, for higher financial returns.

Think of IRAs as vehicles that provide tax advantages for your savings and investments. Different types of IRAs offer different tax advantages and it's important to understand what each type does. There are criteria for qualifying for an IRA, some fees, and, once you put your savings and investments into an IRA, there are limitations and requirements on withdrawals and even penalties. IRAs are available for small contributions, and the SEP-IRA is especially designed for self-employed individuals.

## Investment Warnings and Reminders

With any investment—stocks, IRAs or other, research extensively on your own, and talk to a bank or financial advisor about which directions are best for your income and situation.

When deciding on any investment firm to work with, be sure to do your research on their past performance and their fees. It's even better if you can get a recommendation from someone you know who works with them and has been making money through them. One of the great things about working with a company you trust is that you do not have to know a single thing about investing—if you don't want to. When working with a reputable firm, your money in these types of accounts is carefully managed by experts at the company. And you can decide what and where to invest, or leave it to the company experts to choose whether your money is invested in mutual funds, stocks or other investment options, in this country and overseas. How your money is invested is often based on what Risk Level you are comfortable with.

You need to be planning for the future—and you should start right away if you can. Even if you are very young, time goes by quicker than you can imagine. It is important to start now on your retirement for your survival, health, safety and comfort. If you are middle-aged, many others in your position are just learning about investing. It's never too late to start saving!

It doesn't matter where you are working or how much—or little —you are earning; you still have a shot to go big-time financially and you really do have a choice. Money is money. It doesn't matter where you legitimately earn it. Your dream is worth your hard work. And often a sacrifice now, ends up being a small price to pay for financial peace of mind in the future.

# YOUR PRAISE-WORTHY CONCLUSION
## OF THIS BOOK

It has been such a pleasure guiding and teaching you a system that leaves out all the fluff and semantics and gets you started on a successful career as a singer, songwriter or musician right away.

Please keep an *important* point in mind that I mentioned earlier in this book: if you are stuck in the habit of doing everything for your music career by yourself, you need to learn to *ask* for help from family, friends, colleagues, and those you might hire. You *cannot* wear many hats all the time and successfully alternate them as needed. It is just too much for you to do by yourself.

You are an artist, you are a company, you are *very* special and you need to learn to DELEGATE tasks to other people so that you have more time to work on your music and market it. A lot of people have trouble delegating because they feel they are taking advantage of others, or are simply a one-person business, or that they *should* be able to do it on their own. You know that there are tasks that should be completed by you alone so that you maintain *consistency* in building your career. At the same time, try not to do everything alone. Learn to think like a company, since you *are* a company, and start delegating. If it is uncomfortable for you, then start slowly. You can do it.

I have provided you with a whole book of suggestions—for you and for what you can delegate. And following this conclusion, there are some additional tools to help you in your musical journey.

I am so proud of you and know you will make your music career and quality of life a success, filled with infinite possibilities and happiness. Yes, this is, indeed, the END of the book. It is dedicated to your new *beginning*. Again, be sure you check out the special tools, timeline and tasks in Appendix 1 and the samples of good and bad contracts in Appendix 2, following this conclusion.

Best of luck with your work. I'll be looking for you in the limelight.

*Paul Spencer Alexander*

# APPENDIX 1

## TIMELINE and TASKS

I have given you a lot of information in this book to help you succeed. Though luck does play a part in how successful we are, the best thing you can do to increase the odds of that success is to work hard, passionately, consistently toward your goals. To paraphrase a popular quote: Life—and success—begin at the end of my comfort zone.

I have created a SAMPLE timeline and list of tasks based on what we've learned in this book. As I've said, people work in different ways and at different paces. You are in control, and you can go as fast or as slow as you choose. My suggestion is that you do go beyond what you're used to.

### Beginning

Create a manageable amount of your unreleased songs, CDs and AV files on a computer to release a single song, EP or full album of no more than 10 songs (see Chapter 8).

Or record 3-4 new songs based on the lessons taught in Chapter 8.

Opening a savings account and IRA with low monthly deposits.

## 2-3 months

Build your professional music website before having your music ingested into all digital providers.

Choose web company with built-in blog. See Chapters 13-14.

Make 50 retail CDs.

*Includes:* 50 CD Albums, Full Color Art on CD and cover (if you submit your own artwork), 2 panel sleeve with jewel case shrinkwrap, probably through CD Baby.

Add links to digital sales providers, CD/merchandise links.

On your website, list your bio, live show dates, ticket sales ability, or if you do/don't perform, lots of photos/press about your work.

On your website, add links to your YouTube material ideal.

Get production company name, logo and professional music website URL.

## 4-6 months

Release your single, EP or album on CD Baby or TuneCore into all digital music providers. Have 50 copies made of your CD for retail.

## 6-9 months

Use automated approaches to book your shows online and getting fans, getting your music and bio into as many blogs as possible, via MusicSUBMIT.com or DIY researching/obtaining blog press, or hiring a publicist (not recommended at this time). Promote your music and videos with your own or this book's suggested resources (recommended).

## 9-12 months

Having a person who specializes in writing news-worthy press releases write one and distribute it through an online press release service, if desired, to attract media. Ideally and less costly to you, emailing/calling media yourself to procure press, especially in the age of EPKs. Electronic Press Kits (EPKs) with examples provided in this text and its resources. Start performing regularly if you perform live.

A lifetime...

Healthy habits

## Sample Cost Estimate

Please Note: Website price is roughly $16.95/month for DIY. EPK is $5.00/month or slightly more. Music publicity is $25.00/month...with option of doing single, non-subscription based blasts of your music news/selected digital songs.

Full Year for each service specified above is already included in total cost.

1. Copyrights—Form SR and Form PA, Online Registration--$70.00
2. Bandzoogle Website—Lite $8.29/month, Standard $12.46/month, Pro $16.63/month if annual plan is chosen.

3. CD Baby Pro Album distribution--$69.00
4. MusicSUBMIT.com publicity--$25.00/month
5. 50 Presskits, wholesale--$100.00
6. Tax will always vary according to state. Shipping will vary according to company.

## KEY TASKS TO REMEMBER:

1. 10 song, full-length CD manufacturing and cover design. Quantity: 50 CD Units.
2. Copyright registration online, Form SR to register album. Form PA (please see previous advice in book regarding using or not using this form as secondary form to Form SR. Form SR is most important and perhaps the only form needed at this time.
3. Music website with Bandzoogle.com (recommended, which is geared only to signer/songwriters, musicians and bands. Hostbaby.com, a division of CD Baby, also recommended/geared toward singer/songwriters, musicians and bands, along with other hosting companies from Chapter 2. "Pro Packages" generally include everything along with a built-in blog. Built-in blog is imperative to have.
4. Building your Electronic Press Kit (EPK) with Sonicbids.com, or the company of your choice.
5. MusicSUBMIT.com submission of your required CD and bio materials as needed by MusicSUBMIT. "Best Shot Niche" Package selected. Send EPK if requested.
6. Use automatic gig booking at Sonicbids.com to start playing out, and use your EPK for marketing via email if you make a contact via phone or email. Only send the EPK if contact asks you to.

7. Use EPK for industry opportunities through Sonicbids.com, many resources contained in this book, as well as for worldwide music industry relationships.

8. Build some regular press kits (paper and folder version of your EPK). Folder, bio, good photography, press if any, calendar of shows if any, and CD. Update your website, your EPK and press kit at least once every 2-4 weeks to show that you are a regular, working artist. Go through all the resources in this book and use them to network, create relationships and delegate business tasks to entities.

# APPENDIX 2

## Contracts and Licensing Agreement Samples— Good and Bad

Throughout the book, and especially in Chapter 14, I have talked about contracts and licensing agreements. I've also warned you about unscrupulous people and companies in the music industry who might try to take advantage of you. ALWAYS check with an attorney—preferably one specifically familiar with music-industry legalities—or with the Songwriters Guild—www.songwritersguild.com.

So you at least have an idea of what contracts and licensing agreements might look like—so you better know what to ask the attorney about—I have included some good and bad examples of these.

Disguised as a record contract, this is an attempt to unscrupulously purchase 100% of a song for a flat fee so that they own it. See Chapter 3 on Legal Assistance for reviewing contracts.

Linguistically Deceptive Records
123 Not As Smart Circle
Anytown, CA 54321

## Bad Recording Contract, Example #1

*Filled with misspellings, along with a statement that says that if I don't sign the contract, I must contact them regarding the reason why. I did not contact them. This resulted in a pushy phone call from them. Record companies never call Artists directly. You communicate with them through an Attorney if ANY contract is being addressed or considered.

Paul Alexander

Apt. #205

Mr. Alexander

Thank You for your composition(s); received

*Why didn't they check one of the two sections off? They certainly enjoyed unsuccessful phone efforts to presure me into signing.

___ your work is under review.
___ your work has been accepted for purchase.

Upon finding the appropriate musical composition(s), the composer is contacted by telephone. Our reason is simply to inquire on the composition(s), legal disposition.

After the confirmation is made, then this letter is generated to the compositions' owner.

Mr. Alexander, we offer you:

*Here, this record company deceives the client about giving the client "full recognition" for the work, but and deceptively tries to "buy" 100% of your

1. Full recognition for the musical composition(s) purchased by Linguistically Deceptive Records
2. A cash payment of $250.00 for ownership.

Mr. Alexander, we request from you:
rights to the song as the Songwriter and Performer! In my case, I would have given away a song that's been used in or several projects, all for just $250. That doesn't even take care of the recording costs I incurred in the studio!

1. A letter with yoursignature, signing over, all rights of ownership, to our company.
2. A letter of rejection and your reason why.

Mr. Alexander, should you agree, than a money order will be issued to you, with-in 30 days. Please return your response in the pre-addressed, stamped envelope, as soon as possible.

Thank You

**VOID**

Ex., Officer,
Linguistically Deceptive Records, Inc.

ANY record company that attempts to charge an artist in any way is a SCAM. Avoid.

Bad Recording Contract, Example #2

## RECORD CONTRACT

Whereas **Paul Alexander** is the writer(s) and sole owner of the composition entitled: My Material and Whereas the writer(s) desires the services of
Worst Recording Company.
Now, therefore, Worst Recording Company agrees:

1. To produce high quality compact discs albums entitled "Nothing," containing the above song.

2. To ship 100 of these compact discs containing the above song to disc jockeys, radio programmers and radio stations across the country.

3. To furnish the above writer five of these compact discs for the writer's personal use.

4. To furnish the writer a list of disc-jockeys, radio programmers and radio stations where compact discs were shipped.

And the writer(s) agrees:

1. To provide to Worst Contract* in excellent condition of said song to accompany this agreement if accepted.

2. To pay to Worst Contract the sum of $396.00 for all the above services. Payment may be made in full, or $66.00 with the contract and the balance in FIVE consecutive monthly payments of $66.00 with no interest on the deferred payments. Production of compact disc is to commence upon completion of payments.

3. Writer agrees to complete payment of balance and failure to do so does not entitle writer to a refund, but allows Worst Contract to hold amounts on open account until funds are received and the project can be completed.

4. Writer warrants that composition is his (her) original composition and certifies that he(she) is the owner of exclusive rights.

*You do NOT pay a record company anything out of pocket to "sign you." There are NO exceptions to this rule, ever. This is a SCAM.

**PLEASE READ BEFORE SIGNING:**
*I state that my financial condition warrants my participating in this agreement, and that as a writer I am fully aware that only a small percentage of all songs written become "HITS". It follows that I am aware that songwriting is a high risk venture and that nothing in this contract or any other matter presented to me by Worst Records is regarded by me as a guarantee that my song will earn a profit. However, I do expect Worst Records to fully execute the above agreement, favorable to our mutual benefit.*

*This agreement is made and shall be governed by the Law of the State of California. In order to conform to California Law, persons under 18 years of age accepting the terms of this contract must secure a parent signature. This agreement shall become effective upon receipt by Worst Records* at the home office of Worst Records* Hollywood, California.*
Make sure you ALWAYS read the fine print.

SIGNED AND AGREED:

**VOID**
Worst Records, Hollywood, CA                   Date

**VOID**
Writer(s)                   Date
CD1A
                   Parent Signature

Please sign and return this contract with your payment. A copy of your contract with receipt will be returned to you. California residents add 8.25% Sales Tax.

This is an excellent contract to include a song on a promotional CD. There are no clauses or attempts to take away any publishing rights to the song. See Chapter 3.

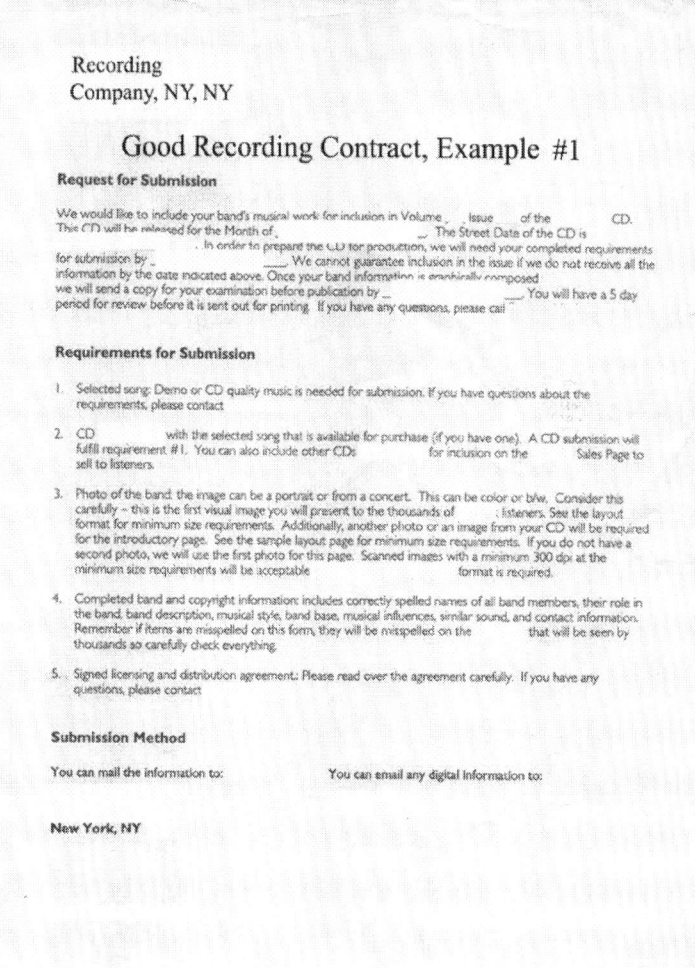

Recording
Company, NY, NY

## Good Recording Contract, Example #1

**Request for Submission**

We would like to include your band's musical work for inclusion in Volume ___, Issue ___ of the ___ CD. This CD will be released for the Month of ___, ___ The Street Date of the CD is ___. In order to prepare the CD for production, we will need your completed requirements for submission by ___. We cannot guarantee inclusion in the issue if we do not receive all the information by the date indicated above. Once your band information is graphically composed we will send a copy for your examination before publication by ___ You will have a 5 day period for review before it is sent out for printing. If you have any questions, please call ___

**Requirements for Submission**

1. Selected song: Demo or CD quality music is needed for submission. If you have questions about the requirements, please contact

2. CD ___ with the selected song that is available for purchase (if you have one). A CD submission will fulfill requirement #1. You can also include other CDs ___ for inclusion on the ___ Sales Page to sell to listeners.

3. Photo of the band: the image can be a portrait or from a concert. This can be color or b/w. Consider this carefully – this is the first visual image you will present to the thousands of ___ listeners. See the layout format for minimum size requirements. Additionally, another photo or an image from your CD will be required for the introductory page. See the sample layout page for minimum size requirements. If you do not have a second photo, we will use the first photo for this page. Scanned images with a minimum 300 dpi at the minimum size requirements will be acceptable ___ format is required.

4. Completed band and copyright information: includes correctly spelled names of all band members, their role in the band, band description, musical style, band base, musical influences, similar sound, and contact information. Remember if items are misspelled on this form, they will be misspelled on the ___ that will be seen by thousands so carefully check everything.

5. Signed licensing and distribution agreement: Please read over the agreement carefully. If you have any questions, please contact

**Submission Method**

You can mail the information to:          You can email any digital information to:

**New York, NY**

If you read numbers 1-6 in the third paragraph, where the 3 red question marks begin, all the way to the end of the third paragraph, most of you would not sign this. Some might. Always consult an attorney when you can. See Chapter 3 for Legal Assistance.

## Bad Music Licensing Deal, Example #1

### AUTHORIZATION TO USE COPYRIGHTED WORK

The undersigned ("Artist") hereby authorizes                     a California
corporation                                 Los Angeles, California        the
non-exclusive right to use the composition and the master recording of the musical composition
embodying the performance of the Artist entitled                     ("Song") in the 1st
installment of
     ("Video").

Artist understands that        is under no obligation to use any or all of the Song in the
Video and no assurances have been given to Artist that such Song will be used. In the event the
Song is used, Artist agrees that he will be paid        and shall receive credits at the end of the
Video which: 1) set forth the name of the Artist who wrote and/or performed the Song; 2)
identify the name of such Song used in the Video; 3) set forth the Artist's affiliation with the
applicable performing rights society; 4) set forth the applicable copyright information; and 5) set
forth the Artist's web site address.

Artist agrees that        shall have the non-exclusive right to use the Song in the Video as
part of the picture on audio/visual devices including but not limited to
     DVDs and similar contrivances whether now known or hereafter devised. Artist
agrees that        shall have the non-exclusive right to use the Song in connection with the Video
so long as the fundamental character of the Song is not altered.        shall have the right to 1)
repeat the Song, or excerpts from the Song, in order to fit the music with the scene; 2) use the
Song in connection with any video image; 3) adjust the volume level of the Song; 4) use all or
just a part of the Song; 5) use the Song multiple times; and 6) use or not use the Song. Artist
agrees that he shall have no right to object to, edit or alter any material which is set forth on the
Video. Artist acknowledges that the Song may be used at any time during the Video and may be
associated with scenes which may or may not be tasteful or provide positive or favorable
association with the Artist.

The Artist retains all rights to reproduce, distribute, perform or display the above Song
and any derivative works based on those Song as well as all other rights, privileges, and remedies
granted or reserved to the Artist under the copyright law of the United States        is not
authorized or permitted to use the song in any manner that is not expressly set forth herein.

Artist represents that it is the owner of the copyrights to the Song and has the full
authority to enter into this Authorization.

Artist:

**???**
"Can you explain exactly what you mean?"

This is a shortened version of a good music licensing contract, due to the length of it. It is good because the company only wanted to use the song in the film. Nowhere in the contract does it try to take away any music publishing rights. You must watch out for these things! See Chapter 3 to review!

## Good Music Licensing Deal, Example #1

### Long Form Master Use License

This Master License dated as of _____ is by and between Paul Alexander ("Licensor") and _____ ("Company") as follows:

1. **Parties**

    a) Company:

    b) Licensor: Paul Alexander

2. **Master**

    The "Master" is that certain master recording of the musical composition entitled _____ (INSTRUMENTAL)" (the "Composition") embodying the performance of Paul Alexander ("Artist").

3. **Picture**

    The "Picture" is that certain motion picture tentatively entitled _____

4. **Use**

    The number(s) of uses, type(s) of uses, and the duration of the uses of the Master in the Picture are as follows:

    Number(s) of uses: 3
    Type(s) of uses: Instrumental Background
    Duration of the uses: Up to the length of the Composition per use

5. **Territory/Term**

    a) **Territory**
    The "Territory" covered by this License is throughout the Universe.

    b) **Term**
    The "Term" of the License is in perpetuity.

6. **Grant of Rights**

    In consideration of the promotional value such exposure will provide the Licensor, licensor hereby irrevocably licenses and grant to Company (its successors licensees and assigns) the perpetual and non-exclusive right...

Example of a Good contract offering Radio Play. There are no hidden clauses or attempts to take away any publishing rights (See Chapter 3); just people who are passionate about some songs they'd love to put on rotation.

# PAUL SPENCER ALEXANDER

Subj:   We're scheduling your music
Date:
From
To:
Sent from the Internet (Details)

### Dear PAUL ALEXANDER

We want to tell you that after listening to the CD "PAUL ALEXANDER"                    we felt very happy with the work and we've decided to schedule it to start in our "New Releases" program, in the air from Jan-24th to Jan-28th, with the introduction of two songs simultaneously.

We ask you to wait, in the next days, for an e-mail with all the details.

We appreciate and respect your job

FM

Rio de Janeiro/RJ

Subj: We´re going to start playing your songs
Date:
From:
To:
File:
Sent from the Internet (Details)

### Dear Sir PAUL ALEXANDER

First of all, we want to thank you once again for having sent us the CD "PAUL ALEXANDER

Now, we want to tell you, and ask you to tell the band, that after listening to the album, we decided to include it, or part of it, immediately in our radio station for airplay. So, we are ready to start playing songs extracted from the album you sent us. Our current airplaying system is the following:

In the first time, the songs selected are played during a whole week, in our program
       FM", (that translated should be                              ), and they are, the same week,
included in our play list, and kept there for 3 weeks more, while, in this period  we´ll keep our
attention in our audience to see their receptivity.

                       is in the air according to the schedule below. It lasts for 60 minutes.
with original presentation on mondays and replayed from tuesday to friday. Therefore the songs, in
realease, will be presented according to this planification, in Rio de Janeiro local time:

| Day of the week | Day of the month | Time |
|---|---|---|
| Monday | 24/01 | 12:00 |
| Tuesday | 25/01 | 14:00 |
| Wednesday | 26/01 | 16:00 |
| Thursday | 27/01 | 11:00 |
| Friday | 28/01 | 13:00 |

OBS.: The schedule above may be changed with no previous advice .

"PAUL ALEXANDER                        will have 2 songs played in each program. The songs from the
album that we are going to be presenting are:

# PAUL SPENCER ALEXANDER

My Song    - track 2

My Song    - track 3

Why those? Simple: we prefer starting by two, and we think they are the best in two different styles, what increases the probability of people agreement

Each one of those songs will be presented once a day, within the        program in the first week and immediately included in our normal program with 2 or 3 inclusions a day, either for the workdays or for the weekends. It´s gonna be at least 60 to 90 airplays this first month.

\* \* \*

     FM station has a privileged localization in Rio de Janeiro     and our audience is ever growing. Our signal, concentrated in the center of most demographic and financial density, reaches the following barrios:

### In Rio de Janeiro city

Centro (downtown), da Cinelândia à Praça Mauá (Centro Comercial/Financeiro - Av. Rio Branco, Rua 1º de Março, Av. Pres. Vargas, Av. Marechal Floriano, Av. Sete de Setembro, Largo da Carioca, Castelo, Praça XV)

Morro de São Bento, Ilha das Cobras, Aeroporto Santos Dumont e aterros (Glória e Flamengo)

Praça da República, Praça Tiradentes e Largo de São Francisco

Cinelândia, Lapa e Bairro de Fátima

Baía de Guanabara e Zona Portuária

Gamboa, Santo Cristo e Saúde

Central do Brasil, Praça da Bandeira, Maracanã, Tijuca

São Cristóvão, Vila Isabel, Rodoviária e Cajú

Cidade Nova, Catumbi e Estácio

Rio Comprido e Cidade Nova

Santa Teresa, Laranjeiras, e Cosme Velho

Gloria, Catete, Flamengo, Botafogo, Humaitá e Urca

### In Niterói city

Centro (downtown), Fonseca, Ingá, Gragoatá, Icaraí, Cantureiro, São Francisco, Charitas, Neves.

# BIOGRAPHY

Paul Spencer Alexander is an international award-winning singer, songwriter, and short filmmaker of pop and rock influenced, visual storytelling. Two of his music films have screened at AMC Movie Theaters, Aventura, Miami. He has over twenty years of experience in writing, music production, performing arts, education and research. He also has a background in Residential Counseling for at-risk youth. Paul began writing songs and music by ear at the age of five. After winning a first place music video performance contest featured in the Village Voice in New York City, Paul auditioned for the IMTA, Los Angeles, taking home a first place prize in team singing, as well as two additional awards for competition excellence in singing and on-camera work. His winnings represented the New York City division of the global competition.

Paul's first music publishing agreement for a single he wrote was included on a CD from a New York City record label sponsored by Armani Exchange. His first musical film that he wrote and directed received press from NBC and ABC online affiliates, with additional praise from other online media. Two of his earlier songs received heavy FM radio play throughout multiple cities in South America. He was awarded a "Best of the Batch" feature from the Music Industry News Network when he released his first official album. His music has also been featured twice in Music Connection Magazine.

Paul began his professional journey with two music industry apprenticeships in college, a promotion to the Board of Directors at a student record label and an award for team leadership during his promotion. He was accepted by audition to the University of Miami Men's Chorale at Frost School of Music, performing around Miami with a group of exceptional singers and musicians. After college, he designed and taught his own songwriting course under the supervision of a music therapy department at a foster home. He has guest taught a variety of academic subjects in public schools, counseled at-risk youth at residential facilities, and created an online music-marketing based resource for artists most in need of knowledge to succeed. Paul is a graduate of the University of Miami, Coral Gables, FL.

Dear reader,

We hope you enjoyed reading *Strike the Right Chord*. Please take a moment to leave a review, even if it's a short one. Your opinion is important to us.

Discover more books by Paul Spencer Alexander at https://www.nextchapter.pub/authors/paul-spencer-alexander

Want to know when one of our books is free or discounted? Join the newsletter at http://eepurl.com/bqqB3H

Best regards,

Paul Spencer Alexander and the Next Chapter Team

Printed in Great Britain
by Amazon